Growing Up Latino

Teens Write About Hispanic-American Identity

By Youth Communication

Edited by Hope Vanderberg

Growing Up Latino

EXECUTIVE EDITORS
Keith Hefner and Laura Longhine

CONTRIBUTING EDITORS
Philip Kay, Tamar Rothenberg, Rachel Blustain, Andrea Estepa, Katia Hetter, Hope Vanderberg, Marie Glancy, Vivian Louie, and Nora McCarthy

LAYOUT & DESIGN
Efrain Reyes, Jr. and Jeff Faerber

COVER ART
Youth Communication Art Department

ISBN 978-1-933939-83-4

Second, Expanded Edition

Printed in the United States of America

Youth Communication®
New York, New York
www.youthcomm.org

Table of Contents

Contents

Contents

Introduction

What does it mean to be a Latino teen? For each of the young writers in this book, the answer is a little different. Their stories take the reader from the U.S. to Latin America and back again as they struggle to figure out who they are.

Some writers, like Sayda Morales in the opening story, "Penguin in the Sahara," are thinking about their Hispanic-American identity for the very first time. Sayda's first year at a mostly-white private school inspires her to go back to her Latina roots. Others, like Charika Martin and David Miranda, write about growing up in an ongoing tug of war between two ethnicities and cultures.

Readers will relate to the fierce pride that many writers take in their culture. Omar Morales wears a Puerto Rican flag necklace to connect with a place that he knows only through stories. And Janill Briones, who is Ecuadorian, is tired of feeling invisible in the Latin American community, where people often assume she is Puerto Rican or Dominican.

Things get more complicated when teens' lives conflict with their parents' ideas of what it means to be Latino. In one story, this means preferring heavy metal music to merengue. In David Miranda's case, it means coming out to his parents, who regularly refer to gay people as "*maricas*" (a derogatory term).

The writers find inspiration as well—in role models from the past, like Puerto Rican baseball player Roberto Clemente, in cultural traditions like Bolivian folkdancing, and in the breathtaking beauty of an ancestral country.

For some, being Latino is about visiting a country they've only heard relatives speak about; for others it's about leaving a native country behind and learning to navigate life in the U.S. When Angy Gonzalez immigrates to New York from Columbia, she pines for her friends back home, while Pedro Cruz hopes never to go back to Mexico after he makes his way through the desert to reach the U.S. In "American at Heart—But Not on Paper," Anonymous lives with the threat of deportation to a country he doesn't even remember.

The writers in this book come from a wide range of Hispanic cultures and experiences. But for all of them, one message is clear: as much as their culture influences their identity, they alone define themselves. We hope their stories will inspire readers to reflect on who they are, and to feel confident that they don't have to fit into anyone else's idea of what it means to be Latino.

Edwin Yang

Penguin in the Sahara

By Sayda Morales

It was my first day of high school and already I felt like an outcast.

I was standing in a corner with the other new girls, marveling at the sight of so many white people. The Nightingale-Bamford School was an all-girls private school on the Upper East Side, one of the richest neighborhoods in Manhattan. It went from kindergarten through high school, which meant most students had already known each other for nine years. As if that didn't intimidate me enough, I was also on scholarship. Most of the other girls were rich, and I mean really rich.

If you had asked me before high school to describe myself in one word, "Hispanic" would have come nowhere near my lips. I attended a public middle school in the South Bronx where most of the students were black or Hispanic like me, and I took my ethnicity for granted. It just didn't seem important. But when I entered private school and found myself in the minority for the first time, I had to figure out what it really meant to be a Latina from the South Bronx.

That first day, I arrived in my navy blue kilted skirt that reached my knees, shoes I got on sale at Macy's and a book bag. Most of the girls wore skirts that ended right underneath their butts, so that you could see their shorts or underwear. They wore Lacoste polo shirts and Coach flats and carried LeSportsac bags. I felt like a penguin in the middle of the Sahara.

Some girls asked me where I lived, and when they heard the words "South Bronx," their eyes widened and their faces elongated in shock. They wanted to know if I had seen people get shot, if I had seen people do drugs, if I had been to any wild parties. I chuckled to myself—did they really think that the South Bronx was that dangerous?

I decided to have some fun with them. I said, "Yeah, I've seen gangsters who kill you so quick, you don't even have time to blink. And drugs? Please, even little old grandmas sell joints. And I never get enough of wild parties; that's all I do on weekends."

It was even funnier to see their gullible faces as they asked, "For real?"

"Uh, no. It was a joke. The South Bronx is about as dangerous as the Upper East Side." (OK, that's not exactly true, but I was frustrated that they thought the Bronx was as dangerous as it's portrayed to be in movies.) It was only 8 a.m. and I was already being exposed to ignorance I'd never thought possible. But what happened later that day was even more eye-opening.

All the girls were crowded into our homeroom; the lights were off and the electronic whiteboard was on. Suddenly, a girl named Vicky walked in and started chanting, "Crank dat Soulja Boy!" Vicky was African-American, but had attended

Nightingale-Bamford since kindergarten. She had a vacation house in the Hamptons and had traveled around the world. In other words, she was nothing like any of the African-American girls I knew from middle school.

Next thing I knew, Soulja Boy's "Crank That" was pumping from the homeroom stereo and girls were imitating the dancing from the music video. I hadn't heard the song before because I didn't listen to hip-hop that much. Out of nowhere one of my new white friends, Delilah, pulled my arm and begged me to dance with her. I shook my head "no" because I had no clue how to crank that soldier boy or even what it looked like. But the other girls started begging me, too, and I was thrust to the front of the room.

I feebly tried to explain I didn't know how to dance to that kind of music, but the girls started saying things like, "C'mon, that's ridiculous. Of course you do!" and, "Just try it, it probably comes natural to you."

It bothered me that my private school classmates didn't recognize my Hispanic culture. Then again, I guess I didn't bother to recognize my Hispanic culture.

I'm sorry to say that I didn't stand up for myself at that moment. I just tried to remember my friend Ashley from middle school, who knew how to dance hip-hop, and I attempted to imitate some of her moves. It was quite pathetic, but surprisingly all the girls thought it was amazing. I was ashamed of myself for trying to fit into their stereotype instead of correcting them.

After that, I became known as the ghetto girl from the ghetto neighborhood with ghetto friends. Delilah would constantly ask me if she was more ghetto than Susie or if Martha was the most ghetto person, as if I was the expert on "ghetto-ness." It didn't really bother me that they called me "ghetto." I figured they associated me with the black girls because I did hang out with the few black students at Nightingale sometimes. But it bothered me that they didn't recognize my Hispanic culture. Then again, I guess I didn't bother to recognize my Hispanic culture.

My mom is from Honduras and my dad is from Mexico. When I was little, we spoke only Spanish at home, ate Mexican and Honduran food, and listened to cultural music. Our lives revolved around Latin American traditions.

But I had slowly assimilated into white American culture over the years. I started listening to pop music and watching American TV shows until my Spanish was terrible and I became too embarrassed to speak it. In kindergarten, before I knew English, my name, Sayda, sounded to me like steamed rice, *platanos* and beans. By the time I entered high school, my name sounded more like hot dogs and hamburgers on the Fourth of July.

After about three months of comments from my classmates, I finally realized that if I didn't stand up for myself and my culture, my classmates would continue to live in ignorance. But what was my culture, exactly?

I started thinking more about everything that made me Hispanic. For example, I still spoke some Spanish and ate Spanish food at home. I danced *bachata* and merengue at parties, and I had been to Mexico and Honduras several times. I was Hispanic at home, but not in school, and I realized that for years, even before high school, I'd been keeping that part of myself separate from who I was at school. But there was nothing to be ashamed of. So what if I watched *telenovelas* as well as *Gossip Girl*? So what if I loved listening to Anthony Santos and Ricardo Arjona as well as 50 Cent and Rihanna?

I began talking to my friends at school about my life and culture. I told them about how I had been in a bilingual class in kindergarten and wasn't fluent in English until 3rd grade. I told them that in my house we eat foods like *platanos, arroz con habichuelas* and *tamales*.

Some girls thought I had an attitude problem and was being arrogant for talking about myself. But the girls who were genuinely interested in learning about Hispanic culture and were sincerely sorry for stereotyping me became my close friends.

I learned to embrace my ethnicity even more by getting involved with school organizations for students of color. That spring, I signed up for a one-day workshop with an organization called Diversity Awareness Initiative for Students (DAIS). Hundreds of other students from private schools in the New York area got together to attend sessions on topics like identity and homosexuality. It was good to talk to other private school students from all different backgrounds who cared about the same issues I cared about.

After that, I joined Cultural Awareness for Everyone (CAFE), a club at my school where black, white, Asian, and Hispanic students come together and talk about our cultures. Talking to other Hispanic students who had gone through similar experiences at my school made me realize I wasn't alone.

My school makes a big deal about African-American History Month, but the most they've done for Hispanic students is celebrate Cinco de Mayo. There's more to Latin America than Mexico. I've made it my goal to educate my classmates about Latin American culture, about how there's a difference between being Honduran and Cuban and Panamanian. And that you can listen to rap or play golf or sing opera, and still be Hispanic.

I don't regret going to private school because I've learned a lot about myself. Going to private school helped me to rediscover who I am and take pride in my ethnicity, and that's the best lesson I could ever learn. Like Gandhi said, I must be the change I wish to see in the world. Recognizing and appreciating my own culture is the first step toward helping those around me see and appreciate my culture, too.

Sayda was 15 when she wrote this story.

Rafael Manashirov

Black? Latina?
Don't Ask Me to Choose

By Charika Martin

My mother's Puerto Rican, but I don't speak or understand Spanish. A few times I went to visit my mother at her job and her Latina co-workers told me how important it was for me to speak Spanish. They pointed at my mother and told her that she should have taught me and my younger sister the language.

I never really understood why she didn't. Then my mother told me that my father, who's African-American, insisted that we only speak English. He didn't understand Spanish and I guess it made him feel stupid when my mother spoke it and he couldn't understand what she was saying.

We grew up living like an African-American family. Besides my mother and older half-sister, who is also Puerto Rican, all the family I knew were black. I was close to my father's family and we would spend Christmas, Thanksgiving, New Year's and birthdays together.

Almost all of my mother's relatives live in Puerto Rico. And although my maternal grandparents often sent my little sister and me cards for our birthdays or money for Christmas, I didn't even know them. I went over there once when I was 2 but I don't remember that at all.

It wasn't until after my parents separated when I was 10 that my mother started bringing up her culture and speaking Spanish more frequently. Then a few years ago I visited Puerto Rico again and got the chance to reunite with my mother's family and become close to my grandparents. I began to realize I was Latina as well.

Before, I had always considered myself African-American even though I knew that I was half Hispanic. But after I realized that I wasn't only black, I wanted others to know too.

I started pretending my last name was Martínez instead of Martin. I remember a girl once said to me in class, "I thought your last name was Martin." I told her it was short for Martínez. I could tell she was annoyed, probably because she thought that I was trying to pretend I wasn't black and show off the fact that I was Latina. I think that she took it as an insult because she was African-American. I guess after all those years of "being" black, I needed some time to "be" Puerto Rican.

But when I began making Latino friends I once again felt that I wasn't Puerto Rican at all. They would start talking about a Spanish ritual that they remembered from childhood that I had never heard of. Or they would say a Spanish word or phrase that had some kind of significance and start laughing and reminiscing about it, and I would feel awkward and different. Since I'm half Puerto Rican I felt like I should know what they were talking about and be able to relate.

I don't think I look Hispanic either. I think I look more like a light-skinned African-American. I have black-textured hair and full lips.

But when I tried to chill with my African-American friends, there were times when I felt different, too. One reason is that I live with my mother, and since my father left seven years ago

I'm only close to her family now. Another reason is that I live in a Hispanic neighborhood; my African-American friends come from other areas.

What made things even more confusing was how people saw me. There were a lot of times when strangers in the street assumed I was Hispanic and spoke and understood Spanish. One time I was standing in front of my school with a Latina friend and a teacher began talking to me about how to keep my leather book bag clean. She started in English and went off in Spanish.

Instead of telling her that I didn't understand, I just nodded my head and pretended I understood. She must have talked for 10 minutes. Luckily, some of the words were in English so I had some idea what she was saying. At least I knew she wasn't asking me a question because if she had, I would've been in trouble.

I felt caught between two different races and cultures. Was there a way to be both without having to deny one or the other?

Another time I was talking to an African-American guy and when I happened to mention my ethnicity, he said, "Oh my God, I had no idea you were half Puerto Rican. I thought you were fully black." Another time I was talking to a Latino guy and he asked me what my race was. After I told him he said, "You don't look black."

"Well I am," I said.

He continued to say, "You don't look black." And I continued to respond the same way. Then I asked him what he thought I looked like, and he said that I appeared to be Dominican.

I had all these people seeing me different ways. I began to feel I didn't know what I was or who I was. I felt caught between two different ethnicities and cultures. I was confused and wasn't sure I wanted to be either one. People kept expecting me to choose.

If I chose to be Puerto Rican, I worried that some African-

Americans would say that I was ashamed of being black. But if I chose to be African-American, the opposite might happen.

So who was I supposed to be? Who was I supposed to act like? Was there a way to be both without having to deny one or the other?

It took me a long time to figure out the answers to these questions. But eventually I understood that the only person I was supposed to be was myself. And the only way I was supposed to act was the way that felt most natural to me.

It took me 17 years, but I learned that there was a way to respect both my heritages. I could dance to rap and reggae and to salsa and merengue as well. I didn't have to choose one over the other. And why would I want to? I'm lucky to be both African-American and Puerto Rican.

Just because I don't speak Spanish yet or look Puerto Rican doesn't mean that I'm not. And just because I don't associate with my father and his side of the family anymore doesn't mean that I'm not still proud to be African-American, because I am.

People sometimes ask me which group I consider myself to be more a part of. "It's hard to choose one ethnicity over the other when I'm both. I can't imagine having to," I tell them. If they then ask me which one I would rather be, I tell them that I'm proud and happy to be both. I wouldn't want to be anything other than what I am.

Charika was 17 when she wrote this story.

Anthone Murphy

Caught in a Tug of War

By David Miranda

Sometimes I feel like a rope in a game of tug of war. On one side is my Dominican mother and her ways. On the other is my Ecuadorian father with his.

Dominicans and Ecuadorians, especially my two families, understand each other about as well as I do trigonometry (not very well at all). Although both speak Spanish, they have different words for things. In Ecuador a jacket is a *chompa* (a Native American word), while in the Dominican Republic it's an *abrigo*. People speak with very different accents, kind of like the difference between an American accent and a British one.

My father's family used to get a big kick out of making fun of the way Dominicans talk. Sometimes they would try to talk like the Dominican campesinos (country people), by imitating the way they "sing" their words.

The problem was, my own mother was a *campesina* and

I didn't find it very funny at all. Talking Spanish around my father's family, I often had to be careful about how I spoke. If I said *"cuidao,"* as my mother says it, they would laugh and say, "The word is *'cuidado.'"* As if I care.

I've heard stereotypes about the two groups for as long as I can remember. My mom often tells me how Ecuadorians are stuck up and are always trying to be better than everybody else. My dad tells me how Dominicans always stick out in a crowd, with their loud cars and the way they dress. He refers to Dominicans as "these people," failing to realize that I am one of them.

Many Dominicans are dark-skinned. Often the Ecuadorian side of my family has tried to put that down by calling me a *cocolo* or n-gger.

One thing that amazes me about Dominicans and Ecuadorians is how, for all their differences, they really are a lot alike. Growing up, there were always big all-night parties several times a year. Any chance we could get, on birthdays, anniversaries or holidays, we would send the invitations and then party until daybreak. Whether it was my mom's or my dad's family, the smell of food would hang in the air and music would blare out.

I noticed the similarities and some differences—even more when I went to visit the two countries as a kid.

My father's family lives in Guayaquil, Ecuador's largest city. Even though the country is very poor, they're middle class. I was amazed by how well they live. When I saw my grandmother's house, I only wished I could live like that. It had three bathrooms and a sunroof with rocking chairs where I spent many a day getting a tan. I also had fun running up and down the stairs. My house in New York City, actually an apartment, doesn't even have stairs.

Every morning I would wake up to the sound of a rooster crowing. Things like that reminded me that I was in a foreign country. Walking along the streets of Guayaquil, I would see kids my age (10 at the time) begging or without homes. The buses were so packed full of people that they would actually be hanging out the doors. I always wondered how the people inside kept from suffocating.

Guayaquil is on the Ecuadorian *costa* (coast). It's very warm and people live much as they live in any other city in the world. In the sierra (mountains), there are very few big cities and many people still live as their ancestors did a thousand years ago. As I drove through the sierra during my visit, I noticed many people dressed in ponchos and straw hats. These were descendants of the old Inca people. I also noticed that some radio stations were not in Spanish; Quechua, the old Inca language, is still spoken in many parts.

I also learned the hard way that many of the native foods are still eaten. One day, my dad, my brother and I stopped along the road to eat. My father ordered us a dish called *cuy* (pronounced kwee). It looked like the roast pig you always see with an apple in its mouth, only much smaller. I refused to eat it. My father told me it was a rabbit, and I finally gave in and tried it.

It tasted oddly like chicken—actually, it was delicious. Afterwards, my dad told me the truth: I had just eaten guinea pig. I was shocked. To this day, I can't look at a guinea pig without feeling guilty.

The thing that stood out most about my visits to my dad's country was the hospitality that everyone showed to us. Everywhere we went they would invite us to this dinner or that. These dinners weren't actually dinners at all, but big loud parties that lasted well into the night.

Another summer, I had the opportunity to visit my mom's country. Arriving in Santo Domingo, the capital of the Dominican Republic, I had memories of Ecuador. The two countries look very much alike. Both were colonized by Spain, so the houses and towns look similar. But in many ways they're also very different.

Driving to my aunt's house from the airport, I knew I was in a tropical paradise, with the Caribbean Sea right there and palm trees looming overhead. But as we drew nearer to my aunt's house I noticed that all was not well in paradise. My aunt lived in a very poor neighborhood near the center of the city.

Santo Domingo looked a lot like any city. It was amazingly dirty, and very hot and humid. The streets were filled with people and traffic. The sound of merengue and other music was everywhere. On the streets were the familiar homeless children I had seen in Guayaquil, only with a darker shade of skin.

Often as I drove around the city with my mom we would pass great luxurious mansions fit for a king, with satellite dishes on top and high fences around them. In these neighborhoods, there was also an unusual number of teens skateboarding. I felt more like I was driving through Southern California than Santo Domingo.

If there is one thing I grew to hate about Santo Domingo, it was the city's electrical system. Sometimes I would be sitting watching TV, and — bam — the lights would go off, and the TV along with them. It was frustrating, but I always had my cousins to talk to. They became my closest friends. I had never met them before, but with all those power outages we had a lifetime to get to know each other.

My mom often tells me how Ecuadorians are stuck up and are always trying to be better than everybody else.

Visiting my grandmother was an unforgettable experience. We drove over high hills, past cows and many pineapple and sugar cane fields to Puerto Plata, a small city about four hours from the capital.

Puerto Plata was very different from Santo Domingo. The streets were clean and there were many resort hotels. We found a place to stay and then set out, up a steep hill overlooking the city, to visit my grandmother. Soon our car would go no farther and we had to walk up the rocky dirt road to my family's house. By now I was tired and hot, and the mosquitoes were killing me (this was before I learned that Calvin Klein's Eternity attracts insects).

As we approached the town, we saw a small boy in tattered clothes. My mom asked him something and he immediately stopped what he was doing and led us to a small wooden shack with a dirt floor and a roof made of leaves. I didn't know any of the people there but it was as if the prodigal son had returned. Everyone was so happy to see us, they were hugging me and overwhelming me with their happiness.

They gave me a ride on a mule and showed me a small stream behind the shack where I went and hung out with my cousins for a while (they kept asking me about New York). My grandmother showered me with all kinds of fruits. As we walked back to the car, I was sad to leave.

Later that night we went to the beach and talked about nothing. We swam next to a beachside restaurant that was playing merengue. Afterward, my aunt and I danced. Watching the sun set, New York felt far, far away.

My mom's culture and my dad's culture do have some differences, but in New York, it's no longer important whether you're from Ecuador, the Dominican Republic, Mexico, or Puerto Rico. Different groups have to learn to work together to survive in a country that is new to them. Here we lose our identities and become Latinos. I don't mind being called that. But I am also Ecuadorian and Dominican, and proud to be both.

David was 16 when he wrote this story. After college, he earned a law degree from The University of Pennsylvania and became a practicing attorney.

See David's story about The Young Lords, starting on p 59.

Thomas Vaughn

When Merengue
Is Just Not Enough

By Karina Sang-Petrillo

I was born in the Dominican Republic but I've lived in the U.S. for seven years. I came here when I was 10 and, according to my parents, I have changed drastically since then. Well, surprise! Mom, Dad, it was bound to happen.

My parents think that most of the changes in my personality and style have been "negative." They blame the society I live in. They think that families in the U.S. are non-functional, that kids don't respect their parents, and that there isn't any communication. They feel this is slowly influencing the way I act. They say that sometimes I'm disrespectful and they blame my quick mood changes on "my bad influences."

My father, especially, used to complain that I was ashamed of my culture and was trying to forget it. I disagree. I have never been ashamed of my culture. It's just that my father and I have different views on what's important. I do have different ideas from him about what it means to be Dominican, but that doesn't mean I'm not proud of my heritage. My mom is more understanding. She realizes that I'm different from them because I'm growing up in a different environment.

Still, both my parents have problems understanding things like why I prefer heavy metal music to merengue, the music from the Dominican Republic. Don't get me wrong, I like merengue. But it's more my parents' music than anything else. I listen to it because they listen to it. I like it but it doesn't speak to my life and my problems the way heavy metal does.

And although my parents have never told me how to dress, my mom sometimes hints about how I used to dress with much more "class" and my dad complains about my miniskirts. I've tried to explain that styles change as a person grows. It's just part of discovering myself. I wear what makes me feel comfortable.

I have other goals in life besides just representing and speaking out for Dominicans. Being successful in my career so I can represent Dominicans in a positive way is the best thing I can do for my people.

I think what my mom misses most is that I used to be an extremely outgoing little girl in my country. When I came to the U.S., I retreated into a shell that I just recently came out of. I was so shy for a few years that my parents didn't know what to do with me. This shell I created was to protect myself from the loneliness I felt when we first came to the U.S. I had problems with students in school who constantly taunted me about my lack of English. It took me quite a while to get over this.

As for my father, he thinks I don't take enough interest in things that are happening to Dominicans right now in the U.S. He says I don't pay enough attention to racism and that I don't want to acknowledge it.

I do know there is racism, lots of it. But I also feel that some people make it seem like an even bigger problem than it is, just to cause more trouble. Every time people from different races are involved in a disagreement, some troublemaker has to come out and make it into a racist incident.

My father says that I'm not facing the truth about how hard it's going to be for me to make it in the world of journalism because I'm Hispanic. Maybe he's afraid that I'll be disappointed. Well, I'm determined to make it, no matter what anyone says.

I have experienced racism, but I have also seen that not every white person is a racist. Racism goes many different ways; it's not just whites against everybody else. Anyone can be a racist. My father can't understand that.

I also think he worries about me forgetting where I come from. He told me about a tennis player who would not tell anyone she was Dominican until people started criticizing her for hiding who she was. I think he's afraid I might do this. He shouldn't be. I don't constantly announce to the world that I'm Dominican, but if you ask me I'll tell you. I am proud of who I am.

But I have other goals in life besides just representing and speaking out for Dominicans. Being successful in my career so I can represent Dominicans in a positive way is the best thing I can do for my people.

Most of the time, I get along great with my parents. We are real friends and I can trust them. But there are a few things that could come between us if we let them, like our disagreement about what it means to be Dominican. Thank God we haven't let these things destroy our relationship.

I only wish my father could understand that just because my interests and goals are different from his, it doesn't mean that I don't love my country and my people.

Karina was 18 and in high school when she wrote this story.

Joseph Perez

Showin' Off My Flag All Proud

By Omar Morales

A couple of years ago, I bought a beaded necklace of the Puerto Rican flag, and once or twice a week I wear the beads around my neck. When I do, I feel more connected with my roots. I feel like I'm a part of something bigger than myself.

When I see other Puerto Ricans showing off the flag, I say to myself, "Yeah, represent." I guess I feel a connection.

But I think I also wear the Puerto Rican beads because in some ways I feel disconnected from my roots. I only know little pieces of our culture.

I've never been to Puerto Rico, and I can't speak Spanish. It would be good to know how to speak the language that my family speaks. Wearing the flag reminds me who I am and where my family came from.

Sometimes, teenagers I've never met pass by me and say things like, "No doubt, kid, showin' off your flag all proud." I just say, "Yeah," and smile for a minute and keep on walking.

In my old neighborhood, in Williamsburg, Brooklyn, where I lived until I was 5, most of the families were Puerto Rican. People were close. They spoke the same language and went to the same small church at the end of my block.

Even after I moved, I went back to visit often because a lot of my family still lived there. It was always fun. I saw the other kids in the street who I'd known for a long time. And every time my family threw a party, whether it was in one of my aunts' houses or a small club, they would start blasting out salsa, merengue or Latin reggae and they would dance all night long. I felt at home there.

But a couple of years ago, after my grandfather died, most of my family who lived in Williamsburg moved out and they live all over the place now.

I've lived in my current neighborhood, which is in between Bensonhurst and Midwood in Brooklyn, for years. There are people from different races and religions, which is good because I get to see how people from different nationalities celebrate their cultures.

It helps to communicate with other people so that there won't be misunderstandings, which is how racism gets started. And at the same time, I see how we are all similar.

But having the people I know move out of Williamsburg also made me feel a little disconnected from Puerto Ricans. So I try my best to learn whatever I can about Puerto Rico.

I listen to some Latin music, and I also listen to a lot of Latin artists who perform songs in English. And any time they are showing a program about Puerto Rico on TV, I watch so I can learn and know all about it.

I've learned about how the indigenous (native) Puerto Ricans lost their land to Spain and then were given to the United States. And I've learned how many Puerto Ricans are also of African descent.

But the main way I know about Puerto Rico is through the stories my mother told me, about when she lived on the island as a teenager for a couple of years.

She told me that inside the house, they put nets over the bed whenever it was time to go to sleep to keep insects and other small animals away. She described how frogs and small lizards would run around the house. Having a bunch of frogs and lizards running through the living room sounded fun to me.

My mother also told me about the small bridge that she and my uncles used to cross. The bridge was very thin and only two people could cross at a time because it couldn't hold too much weight.

Stories like that fascinated me and made me more interested in visiting the island. I'm not sure I'd want to live there permanently. I'm already used to living in New York with the crowded streets and trains. But in the future, I hope to visit the island and see how it really is.

Until I do, wearing the beads gives me some kind of bond with other Puerto Ricans. Wearing them makes me feel like I'm part of a family.

Omar was 19 when he wrote this story.

Kenly Dillard

Don't Call Me Puerto Rican

By Janill Briones

When I was in 7th grade, our principal asked me, my best friend Tatianna, and another friend if we wanted to ride on a float in New York City's annual Puerto Rican Day Parade. The three of us had the highest grades in the entire 7th grade, and since we were all Hispanic, we were given this opportunity.

"I don't think I want to go," I told the principal.

He looked at me oddly. "Why not?" he asked. My friends were looking at me, waiting for a response.

"Well, I'm not Puerto Rican, so I shouldn't be on the float." I was afraid I might sound a bit childish, but I felt that I had to stand up for my heritage; my family is from Ecuador.

"But that doesn't matter," he said. "The only thing that matters is that you're Hispanic."

That bothered me even more. It was as if the principal, who's

31

white, was saying that all Hispanics are represented by Puerto Ricans, or that all Hispanic cultures are the same. We all speak Spanish, but that doesn't make our cultures identical.

It's bad enough that when people meet me, they often assume I'm Puerto Rican or Dominican. By wanting to include me as a non-identified Ecuadorian in the Puerto Rican Day parade, I felt that my Ecuadorian heritage was being made invisible.

"No, I don't want to go. You should just find someone else," I said.

I didn't go to the parade, but Tatianna and my other friend did, along with another girl who took my place; all three are Puerto Rican.

It might have been fun to be on a float in a parade, but I don't regret passing on it. I was able to stand up for the country that defines part of who I am. Both sides of my family are from Ecuador, and every couple of years, we visit our relatives there. I take pride in my Ecuadorian heritage.

There's an Ecuadorian Day parade in Queens, New York in August. It's not as big a deal as the Puerto Rican or Dominican parades, where stars like Jennifer Lopez join in and celebrate. Our parade is mentioned once on the 11 o'clock news and that's about it.

I like to watch the small floats go by, though. It feels nice being surrounded by a whole bunch of other Ecuadorians, some waving huge flags of yellow, blue and red. It's my community.

I feel that my heritage and my family's traditions get ignored when people assume I'm Puerto Rican or Dominican. But it's true that Hispanic countries have some similarities.

Spain conquered the Native Americans in much of Latin America—the Caribbean, Mexico, Central America and South America. For that reason, Ecuador, like Puerto Rico and the Dominican Republic, is mostly Spanish-speaking and the people practice Roman Catholicism.

My mom is especially religious. She prays every day, and when I don't want to go to church, she starts rambling on about how my cousins in Ecuador love to go to church.

When I go to Ecuador on vacation, Mom has me sit through a *velorio*; that's basically a reunion among family and friends where everyone sits around a bunch of saint statues and prays. Sometimes it's for somebody who died, sometimes just for the well-being of our families. It's incredibly boring because I'm not that religious, but I go through with it for my relatives.

But Ecuador's geography and history are different from that of both Puerto Rico and the DR, which are Caribbean islands. Ecuador is in South America, straddling the equator and lying between Colombia and Peru.

If I'm lucky enough to get a window seat on the flight to Ecuador, I get to see the country's landscape: the snow-capped Andes mountains and the Amazon River.

When we go to the beach on the weekend, I look at the Pacific Ocean and envy the Ecuadorians for their clean water and their empanada and ice cream vendors. It's so much better than the beaches we have in New York where I live.

Some people have said to me that if I don't eat rice and beans, I'm not Hispanic. But that's not what we eat—and of course I'm Hispanic.

There's a restaurant at the beach that serves delicious *ceviche*, which is cold, spicy seafood marinated in lime juice. At home, Mom cooks mostly fish dishes, too, like fried fish and fish soup.

Some people (usually Dominican or Puerto Rican) have said to me that if I don't eat rice and beans, I'm not Hispanic. But that's not what we eat—and of course I'm Hispanic.

Ecuador's population of nearly 14 million is ethnically mixed. There are more than 10 different indigenous (native or Indian) groups, as well as white (mostly Spanish) and black Ecuadorians. Mestizos, who are a mixture of indigenous and white, make up 65% of the population.

I think that I have a mestizo background, though I don't

know for sure. My family speaks Spanish, not an indigenous language like Quechua. My grandfather from my mother's side has blue eyes, like some Ecuadorians do. Most of us have brown eyes though, and my dad's family has darker complexions, so I think it's likely that some of my ancestors were indigenous.

My father came to the United States to find work soon after my parents got married. After a couple of years, my mom was able to join him here. Since money was an issue back in their day, they had to work hard to put food on the table. My dad says that we're better off here than in Ecuador.

Over half the people in Ecuador either live in poverty or are really close to it. Like most immigrants, Ecuadorians have moved to the U.S. to make a better life for themselves. Ecuadorians now make up 43% of all South Americans in New York, and 5% of New York City's Hispanic population.

Belonging to a small community does have its positive side. I could consider myself a rare species.

That's more Ecuadorians than I expected when I first started my research. The part of Brooklyn where I live seems to be made up of mostly blacks, Orthodox Jews, Puerto Ricans and Dominicans, though I do know a few Ecuadorians in my building and a few others in the neighborhood.

There are many more Puerto Ricans and Dominicans than there are Ecuadorians in the New York City area. Put together, they make up over half of the Hispanic population.

Since there are so many Puerto Ricans and Dominicans in New York, they've become an important part of the city's life and history.

Puerto Ricans especially have been in New York for a long time. Puerto Rico is actually a part of this country; it became a commonwealth of the U.S. in 1952.

Between 1945 and the 1960s, huge waves of Puerto Ricans

immigrated to New York, mostly looking for better opportunities and employment.

The Dominican wave of immigration to the U.S. didn't happen until 1961, when the dictator who ruled the DR was killed and it became easier for Dominicans to leave the country. Thousands of Dominicans came to New York, for mostly the same reasons that Puerto Ricans did.

It makes sense that Puerto Ricans and Dominicans have a big New York presence, but we Ecuadorians may be catching up.

Last year, while I was working on my Halloween decorations and my brother Ronald was playing video games, he told me about school that day. His teacher had asked the class to name as many Hispanic countries as they could. He said that, to his great shock, Puerto Rico and the Dominican Republic weren't the first ones that people named.

"Yo, I couldn't believe it; they were like the last ones that were named. I was mad happy," he said, turning back to his game.

I felt happy, too, even though Ecuador wasn't the first country named, either. It felt like we had won a mini-battle that nobody else knew about. (Maybe I just have an ill mind).

Belonging to a small community does have its positive side. I could consider myself a rare species. I do get a thrill out of knowing that people never know I'm Ecuadorian until I tell them; it's like my secret identity. And I guess what really matters is that I know where I'm from.

Janill was 17 when she wrote this story. After high school, she went on to study animal behavior at Hunter College in New York City.

Nelle McKay

No Poofy *Quinceañera* Dress for Me

By Daniela Castillo

My 15th birthday was nearing and I was getting nervous. For the last few months, I'd been getting pressured from both sides of my family to have a *quinceañera* (keen-sen-**ye**-rah).

My mom is from Venezuela and my dad is from Spain, two cultures that are strict believers in *quinceañeras*—big celebrations that Hispanic families throw on a young woman's 15th birthday to celebrate her transition into womanhood. It would be a day of eating and dancing where family members would get to see me in all of my "poofy dress" glory.

My mom and her five sisters all had pretty decked-out *quinceañeras* in the 1960s. Their parties were held in big ballrooms in Venezuela with music and fashionable dresses.

All of my aunts have given me different accounts of the

"best night of their lives" to get me to have a *quinceañera*. On my father's side, my female cousins called from Spain to convince me that I'd get a lot of presents and be pampered for the day.

W hy wouldn't I want a big party thrown for me? One reason is that I'm just not a party person. My idea of a good time is going with some friends to see a cool movie or just hanging out at each other's houses.

But it's not just the tacky frills and bows of *quinceañera* that I don't like. It's also the money. I know families that spend thousands of dollars on *quinceañera* parties just so their kids can show off to their friends.

One of my cousins in Spain rented out a mansion in Barcelona and invited most of her town to the party. Making *quinceañera* all about who can spend the most money takes away from the purpose of the tradition—to show you're mature and ready to become more responsible.

My relatives made it seem like I'd been a burping, ball-scratching man before, and through the miracle of a quinceañera, I had been transformed into a princess.

I also hate that the birthday girl wears the biggest, pinkest and most uncomfortable-looking dress ever made. Not that I'd change my mind if I could wear jeans and Nikes. I still wouldn't like the weird ritual that gave my nosy family members an excuse to humiliate my cousins at their quinceañeras and make them feel uncomfortable.

I saw the humiliation first-hand two years ago, when I went to my cousin Genesis's quinceañera at a restaurant in Queens, New York. I was told I was going to be a special guest, which is really like the maid of honor for quinceañeras. At the end of the night, I'd hand her a candle and a rose, and say a little speech congratulating her on this momentous occasion and wishing her the best of luck.

I followed her the whole night and witnessed all of our family asking her if she had a boyfriend and what size bra she wore. I could see her perspire through her rose pink satin gloves from sheer embarrassment. Knowing the same humiliation would be repeated if I had a quinceañera, I decided to not have one.

I could already see my family scrutinizing me and thinking about what I should be doing now that I'd turned 15. How I must be liking boys or wanting a boyfriend and how I had to start wearing dresses and heels and giggle a lot, like my cousins who are considered pretty and ladylike do.

About 80% of the pressure came from my mom's mother. My grandmother is the best for typical grandmother reasons: she defends me when my mom is yelling at me, she spoils me rotten and she lets me be whatever I want to be.

Having my family respect my decision made me feel like their equal, not like a kid they could pick on.

So it came as a surprise when she was the one who was hovering over me every day, asking me about the plans for my quinceañera. It had been a special occasion that she'd celebrated with her daughters and now she wanted to share it with me. She tried to negotiate with me. Knowing I hated wearing dresses, she said I didn't have to wear a dress as long as I had a party.

I understood my grandmother's reasons. And I would have loved to see both sides of my family at my birthday party—but I also wouldn't be able to stand having them in the same place. My mom's Venezuelan family is loud and sometimes obnoxious. If the music is not ear-bleeding loud, it's not a party. My dad's Spanish family couldn't be more different. They're an old-school European bunch. They're really proper and prefer a quiet family dinner to an all-out party.

And since every Hispanic party calls for some drinking, these differences get multiplied ten-fold. The most hilarious example was at a New Year's Eve party at my father's sister's house in Connecticut about three years ago. My mother's brother Oscar drank too much and collapsed while dancing with one of my aunt's fancy friends, who ended up with a broken wrist. My aunt was furious and threw him out of the house, so we had to leave the party early.

Five months before I turned 15, I told my mom I didn't want a quinceañera. I didn't want her spending money on something I knew I wasn't going to enjoy. I jokingly told her I would rather she give me the money that she would spend on a party, and just have a small family gathering. She said she didn't have a problem with my decision, but warned me about the fit my grandmother was going to have.

Her family in New York and Venezuela started flipping out when they found out. They said they wanted me to continue this tradition. They were bummed out that I was passing up the chance to meet distant relatives from Venezuela and Spain who would fly into town and give me a lot of money.

One of my cousins had gotten at least $6,000 at her quinceañera, not to mention the clothes and gift certificates. I didn't care. All those presents came at a price—getting humiliated by the family—that I wasn't willing to pay.

In the end, I decided to have a 15th birthday party that I refused to call a quinceañera. It was a small family reunion at my house, although my mom went overboard as usual. We had most of the food catered, but my mom still made five giant trays of her signature lasagna and potato salad, which I helped make the day before. My mom's friend's nephew is a DJ so he brought over his equipment and played music for the night.

I'd sent invitations out and told my mom to tell people it was a casual reunion, so nobody showed up in evening gowns and complicated hair do's. There was no fancy giant chair where I'd have to sit all night. Only five of my close friends came and the rest were family members.

My favorite aunt, Carmen, flew in from Venezuela and even my dad's mother from Spain came. My Spanish grandmother gave me the best present of the night—a portrait of her when she turned 15. She's mute, so I've never had a conversation with her. But I've been dying to because she seems like she's got some stories to tell.

It was like she was trying to connect with me by giving me the picture. It was in an intricate wooden frame, and she's looking up to her right with this gorgeous mane of dark hair over her shoulders. I told her that she was quite the looker in her day, and she laughed and laughed.

The lack of flash kept my nosy family members from humiliating me too much. They did tell me how I was looking prettier already and how I was a young lady now and had to behave accordingly. They made it seem like I'd been a burping, ball-scratching man before, and through the miracle of a quinceañera, I had been transformed into a princess. It didn't matter that I wore my regular get up of jeans, a T-shirt and sneakers.

The highlight was when a mariachi band came out of nowhere and started serenading me. (I found out later that the band was my dad's idea to embarrass me.) The lead singer in the mariachi band was really drunk, and everyone knew it. I had to stand there politely and stare into his bloodshot eyes as he sang to me, while people around me tried to contain their laughter.

In retrospect, my party was a nice experience. I got to hang out with my friends and introduce them to the craziness that is my family.

When I took control of my party, I think I demonstrated the maturity symbolized by a quinceañera. I showed determination. I didn't whine or complain. I gave clear and sensible reasons why I didn't want one, just like a lady would. Having my family respect my decision made me feel like their equal, not like a kid they could pick on. And I have to admit it was fun counting the cash with my mom at the end of the night.

Daniela was 15 when she wrote this story.

Gerald Page

I Hated Myself

By David Miranda

By the time I was 11, I already knew I was gay and I hated myself for it. I hated myself so much that I wanted to kill myself. I wanted to be "normal." I didn't want God to punish me and give me AIDS. I didn't want to go to hell.

Every day after school I would go to church. "Please give me the strength to change myself," I would pray. "Please, please, please." I always expected God to answer me but She or He never did. I remember one day at school one of the kids in my class asked a teacher, "Does God always answer your prayers?" The teacher replied, "Yes, no matter what, in one form or another God will always answer your prayers." Not mine.

I even made a vow that if God would make me heterosexual I would become a priest. After church I would go home and read the entire Bible. All I remember about being 11 is praying. Every Saturday I went to confession. I would confess everything except that I had gay feelings. On Sundays I made sure I went to mass. None of it worked.

"Why me?" I'd ask myself over and over again. I saw myself as a freak of nature, and as a devil. All that I ever knew about gay men at the time were the stereotypes and lies that my parents had taught me: That they were child molesters and wanted to be women.

"*Siéntate bien*," my father would tell me. "*Camina como hombre.*" ("Learn how to sit right. Walk like a real man.") He said these things to me so many times that I can still hear him.

My parents taught me that gay people were not people at all. Driving through the West Village neighborhood in Manhattan, I remember them laughing at the "*maricas*," and trying to imitate gay people by saying, "*Ay, chus,*" and acting like stereotypical homosexuals. This taught me that gay people didn't deserve any respect. So how was I supposed to feel when I discovered that I was gay? How is one supposed to feel when you find out that you are a freak, a pervert, a piece of human crap?

One day I told my friend, John (not his real name), that I was planning to kill myself. I asked him how I should do it.

"Why don't you try mothballs?" he said. John was supposed to be my best friend. I figured that if my best friend didn't care whether or not I died then no one else would either. I knew that I was alone and that there was no one I could turn to. I was scared of people.

That's when I made up my mind to do it. I was scared and felt I didn't deserve to live. It was as if there was a knife lodged in my chest that I couldn't take out. I thought about different ways to kill myself. I went to my roof and looked down but I was too scared to jump. I figured that Windex could kill a person, so I drank a whole bottle. It didn't even make me sick.

Then I decided to swallow a whole bottle of Tylenol. I drank it down with iced tea, and every time I took another pill I felt glad that I was that much closer to death and that much further from having to live a miserable life. I closed my eyes and went to sleep hoping it was all over and I'd never have to wake up again.

All I remember from that night was waking up in the darkness every half hour to throw up. I felt as if there was some monster inside of me that just wanted to come out. I remember leaning over the toilet bowl and feeling dirty, and hearing my father say, "Let it out, let it out, you'll feel better." But I just kept throwing up over and over again.

The next morning when I opened my eyes, I felt as if I had spent a night in hell. I realized that nothing had changed. I still had to deal with my stepmother who was always hitting me, and on Monday I'd have to deal with the jerks at school again who always brought up the word, "f--got."

I went to a guidance counselor and, without telling her that I was gay, told her what had happened. I made up a story about a friend dying. By that time I already knew that the best way to keep my secret was by lying.

The counselor called my father and he rushed to school. She told me to step outside while she talked to him. I waited anxiously outside wondering what my dad would do when he came out.

My parents taught me that gay people were not people at all. So how was I supposed to feel when I discovered that I was gay?

Instead of yelling at me, my normally grumpy father was nicer than I'd ever seen him before. "You're my son and I love you," he told me. "Why would you do something so stupid?" I could tell that he was trying to do everything in his power not to upset me. In a way I was glad because he was giving me a lot of attention. He took me out to eat, and talked about moving out of New York City. But in another way it felt so fake that it made me uncomfortable.

The guidance counselor told him that I needed to go to the hospital, because there was a possibility that the Tylenol could have done physical damage. At least that was the excuse that they gave me to convince me to go to a psychiatric hospital for three months.

I will never forget the fears that went through my mind when they told me I would have to go to a mental hospital. I imagined a place full of crazy people who would try to hurt me. I also imagined a deranged psychiatrist who would put doses of harmful medication in my food.

But the three months that I spent at the hospital were actually fun. I woke up every morning and went to group meetings and activities. It was the first time that I actually had friends. Up to that time I had tried my hardest to avoid other people my age. I felt that nobody would like me. I hated people.

At the hospital I was with people who actually liked me. They were all older, about 16 or 17, and to them I was the cute little kid. I enjoyed the way they were treating me. During meals we would talk and I would laugh. I know that doesn't sound like much but laughing and being happy was a rare feeling for me in those days. At the end of each day we would go to the gym and work out. It was all a lot of fun. And my parents were nicer to me than they had ever been before.

I went home and swallowed another bottle of Tylenol, for no reason other than to make myself suffer through another hellish night.

After three summer months I was out of the hospital. I had lied my way through the whole therapy, saying that my only problems were my best friend who had committed suicide, the fact that I had no friends, and that I hated myself. The one time the subject of homosexuality came up I just said, "It's weird. I don't understand how anyone can not like women." They believed everything and then sent me to live with my mother in Brooklyn.

In Brooklyn I found new friends. I continued to live a lie, however. One day I went home and swallowed another bottle of Tylenol, for no reason other than to make myself suffer through another hellish night. Another time I took 20 of my mother's blood pressure pills. I felt that I had no reason to live. My vision of myself as an adult was as a lonely miserable person who would never be accepted by society. The idea of dying in my sleep was very attractive.

I would go to school and chill with my friends and we'd lie to each other about how many girls we'd had. I got into a lot of fights because at that age kids would call each other f--got. I would get extremely offended by this word, and I would beat up anyone who said it to me. Some of my friends would ask me, "Why do you get so offended when people call you f--got if you know you're not?"

I would ask myself how did they know what I was or was not. I was still afraid to admit to myself that I was gay. I started asking girls out, and lying to myself by telling myself that girls were my thing. I started to date them and I enjoyed it. I enjoyed them as far as friendship was concerned but I didn't see it going beyond that.

*J*unior high school was a total flop for me. I did everything to prove my manhood. I stole cars, picked fights, and went on rampages in the train, "catching herbs" with older kids and cutting school. I went from the class nerd to the most likely to drop out.

I got out of it all when I decided to go to a high school that was outside my neighborhood. All of my "friends" were going to the neighborhood high school, so I now had the chance to go and make some new friends in a place where nobody knew anything about me.

On my first day a question was haunting me: "What if people find out?" I was terrified out of my mind.

At first I made many friends but then I would close up and stop talking to them. I was so afraid of being found out that I would stop going to school just so that I didn't have to deal with people.

When I did go I started monitoring my every move. I was scared to talk, walk, or even look at anyone. I felt as if I had the word "f--got" stamped on my forehead.

Eventually I was put in "holding power," which is a nice way of saying truant class. I was just waiting for my 16th birthday so that I could drop out.

I t was during high school that I found that I needed a place to meet other gay people. I knew there were places like that out there, but I didn't know how to get in touch with them. I decided that I was going to ask a guidance counselor for places to go. I wasn't sure whether it was the right thing for me to do. I kept thinking about it for weeks. What if he called my parents? What if he laughed at me? What if they threw me out of school?

Finally I arranged to talk with a guidance counselor. My heart raced and my palms were sweaty as I prepared to tell the first person ever about my big secret.

"How can I help you?" Mr. Smith, my guidance counselor, asked me.

"I have a very big problem," I said. Then came the big bomb: "I think I might be gay."

He just smiled and said, "And?"

My first thought was, "Is this a joke?"

All at once I was relieved and shocked to find that the first person I told didn't freak out. The experience gave me a lot of confidence. It helped me to realize that I was being too hard on myself.

Mr. Smith told me about the Hetrick-Martin Institute for Gay and Lesbian Youth. At HMI they had an after-school center where I met other gay and lesbian teens. I couldn't believe that there were other people out there who were going through the same thing I was.

At Hetrick-Martin I got to know kids from all over New York

City, and of all races. It didn't matter that everyone was gay. What mattered was that everyone was cool. It was a place where I didn't have to hide who I was and where I could just be myself.

At first I kind of felt uncomfortable being around other gay people. The trouble was that after pretending to be somebody else for so long I really didn't know who I was. The only thing I had thought about since I was 11 years old was what was I going to do about this gay crap. I didn't know how to think about anything else.

Then I found that I was not only gay, I also liked to have fun. I liked to go to the movies. I liked to hang out and chill with my friends, and I loved to listen to music. I was smart. I liked to do things that anybody else liked to do. I was a human being just like everybody else; I just happened to be gay. I didn't admit that to myself until I was 14.

At first I kind of felt uncomfortable being around other gay people.

It was around this time that I started my first relationship. His name was Chris. I met him at HMI and I found that I liked talking to him. We would hang out with our friends, go to clubs or just chill and talk. I found that with Chris I felt happier than I had ever felt with any girl. Our relationship was totally based on friendship and respect.

Through all of this I was still cutting school, and my mom would get suspicious about me hanging out late at night. Sometimes I would come home high on an acid tab and try to act as if I wasn't high. I didn't care anymore about school. My only concerns became clubs, my friends, and hanging out.

Finally my mother got fed up with everything and kicked me out of my house and sent me to my father's house. She told me I would amount to nothing and that I would be a bum when I grew up.

I hated my father's house. He would put so many restrictions on me that I wasn't used to. I had to be home by 11:30 p.m. If I wasn't home my father would yell and scream and let me have it. I hated having to put up with that. It was around this time that I was trying to let my parents know that I was gay. I was fed up with living a lie, and I was fed up with having to lie to myself or anyone else about what I was.

One day I arrived home and my father was sitting on the couch watching TV. It was a Friday night and it was only 10:30. "Where were you?" my father yelled.

"I was out," I told him.

"What were you doing?"

By this point I was quite angry. I mean, who did this man think he was to be screaming on my time? I wasn't a little kid, and I was sick and tired of him telling me how to act, what to do, when to do it, and with whom. So I told him that it was none of his business where I was and that he should stay the hell out of my life. That got him very upset.

All of a sudden he grabbed me. "Goddamnit, you're my son," he said, "and I want to know what you're doing." He started to cry and demanded I tell him if I was using drugs, if I had a girl-friend, a job. But the question that really hurt me was, "Are you a f--got?" It wasn't so much the question itself as the way he asked me. He had the most hateful look on his face, as if he were liter-ally ready to kill someone.

"Let me get the f-ck out of this house," I yelled. "I don't want to live here anymore."

"You're not leaving this house until you tell me what you're up to," he said.

"Let me go or I swear I'm going to jump out of that window," I replied. The only problem was that the window was five stories up, and I meant what I said.

He started to grab me and hit me. I was screaming and telling him that I was going to kill him. I was actually very scared. He kept telling me to shut up because the neighbors were listening. I told him I wanted them to hear. I wanted to kill him. I wanted to open the door and leave but he wouldn't let me.

My heart was beating fast and I was gasping for air and crying. I pushed him away, ran for the window, opened it, and was ready to jump, when my father grabbed me. He became afraid for me, and he said that he was very sorry and begged me to forgive him. I said that it was alright.

The next day was Saturday and my father called me from his job and told me in a really nice way that in the afternoon we were going to the doctor. I asked why. "You know, just to get a check-up," he said. Later in the day he came to pick me up. When we walked into the office the doctor asked me, "So what's the problem?"

"This ain't a doctor," I thought. "This is a therapist." I was upset that my father had lied to me and afraid that I would have to spend more time at the hospital. The doctor recommended to my father that I be admitted to Jacobi Hospital. Once I got there they took a lot of blood from me, and then locked me up in a glass room with a man who smelled really bad and who kept talking to himself. Then they gave me some nasty food.

I was scared to talk, walk, or even look at anyone. I felt as if I had the word "f--got" stamped on my forehead.

Later they made me talk to a social worker. He kept asking me what was wrong but I wouldn't tell him. I didn't tell him anything, but he still felt that he had the right to tell my father that he thought I was gay.

After a few hours I was sent to another hospital in the Bronx just for teens and then, after about a week, transferred back to the hospital I had been in when I was 12. My father and mother would talk to me about how much they loved me and how they would support me in anything I did.

I felt angry and confused because I had never told them

anything or officially "come out" to them—someone else had. I felt bad that my parents had to go through all this. I knew they were sad and that they didn't want me to be gay. To be honest, if I had a choice I wouldn't have chosen to be gay either. Who in the world would choose to go through all the name-calling, all the bashings, and all the other crap gay people have to go through every day?

But in a way I was glad that my parents found out while I was in the hospital because I didn't have to go through the "coming out" experience by myself. I had social workers and other people there for me. We would have family therapy where they would put my mother, father and me with a social worker to talk about what life would be like for me when I left the hospital. It was agreed that I would go back to live with my mother, and a contract was drawn up about what the rules would be.

Asking for help and coming out were two big steps toward learning to accept myself.

My parents and I would have heated arguments about what school I would go to and about my being gay. I told them it wasn't any of their business who I slept with. They disagreed and said I was just confused and that I would grow out of it. They would talk to me about AIDS, trying to scare me into not being gay.

I told them that I already knew a lot about AIDS and ways to prevent getting it. They acted as if I was stupid and didn't know anything. I would tell them about ways you can and cannot get it, and that if I had sex I would always use a condom no matter what the circumstances. I also told them that I was not sexually active, which was true. They acted as if I would get AIDS from the air just because I was gay. They were so ignorant in so many ways.

M y mother and I would talk about what my being gay meant to our relationship. I explained to her that I was still the same person and that it didn't matter. My mother would tell me that she was upset because she was not going to have any grandchildren from me. That made me angry. "Who are you thinking about," I asked her, "you or me?"

After two months I left the hospital and went to live with my mother. I decided to go to the Harvey Milk School, a high school for gays, lesbians and bisexuals, and things have gotten a lot better since then. I have plenty of friends and am happy with my life. Coming out to my family was hard but, now that I have, I can tell my parents almost anything and they give me all the support in the world. I'm also involved in a lot of political causes. And I'm graduating this month and will be going to Antioch College in Ohio.

I know now that I didn't really want to die. If I had, I never would have been able to accomplish any of these things.

If you're feeling suicidal you should talk to someone—guidance counselors, friends, family, there are even special hotlines. Suicide is no way out.

What I really wanted was to live in a world where I wouldn't have to deal with people's prejudices. For me, asking for help and coming out were two big steps toward learning to accept myself. I'm not going to let other people's stereotypical perception of gay people put me down.

David was 17 when he wrote this story.

Remy Whitacre

Grandma, I Love You

By Daniel Rosado

Recently, as I was sitting on a park bench catching my breath after a bike ride, I noticed an elderly man sitting close by me. He acknowledged me with a friendly smile. We began to talk to each other about nothing in particular—how beautiful the weather was and how well our favorite sports teams were doing this year. When he told me that he was waiting for his "wonderful grandchildren," I started to think about how important he must be to them. As I left the bench and continued on with my bike ride, I started to think about how important my own grandmother is to me.

I rode across the hills of the park thinking about the summers of my childhood—when my grandmother lived in Puerto Rico and I would go to visit her. I thought back to a cloudy day in Puerto Rico when I was 7 years old. I had just gotten off the airplane with my older brother and was anxiously looking through the crowded San Juan airport for my grandmother's familiar face.

"Look, there's Mama," my brother yelled enthusiastically. Before my grandmother could see us, I ran toward her and tugged at her dress. She turned around and her face lit up with instant happiness.

During the three-hour drive from San Juan to our family's property in the town of Isabela, my grandmother, my brother and I spoke about how we had missed each other. My brother and I hadn't seen our grandmother since the previous summer, so we had a lot of catching up to do.

As the clouds faded away and exposed the sun, we found ourselves in our hometown. When we got to the house, I saw my grandmother's four brothers and her sister waiting for us on the balcony. It was a shock to see them there because they all lived in different towns and didn't get together that often. I was elated that my grandmother had arranged to have them all waiting to greet us.

That first day back in Puerto Rico felt too good to be true. We all ate *arroz con pollo* (chicken and rice) that one of my uncles had prepared and spoke about the family in New York and how we were managing there. Everything was perfect. But that night, I started to feel homesick. I couldn't sleep and I began to cry, complaining that I missed my mother.

I got up and walked into the dark living room, followed by my grandmother. She sat on her rocking chair and put me on her lap. She began singing an old song that went: "My baby lies over the ocean, my baby lies over the sea. Oh bring back, bring back, bring back my baby to me."

Hearing her sing that phrase repeatedly with her cute broken English made me feel so safe and secure. The thing I remember most about those summers in Puerto Rico is how she always found a way to cheer me up when I was uneasy about something.

I have come to appreciate my grandmother even more since

she came to live with my mother, my brother, and me. In the seven years since she moved to New York, she has become like a second parent to me. When my mother goes to work, my grandmother cooks food for the family (the best food I've ever tasted) and usually does the laundry.

Over the years, we've watched each other grow and learned a lot from one another. I've taught her to watch Spanish soap operas (she never watched TV back in Puerto Rico) and she has taught me not to talk to my mother until after she is through eating—she usually gets tired after a hard day's work and wants to be left alone for a while.

I respect my grandmother above anyone else in my life. She is a genuinely good-hearted person who always helps me out if I get into a dilemma. For example, it was because of her that my brother never caught me sneaking out of the house with his clothes on. Whenever he noticed that something of his was missing, my brother would ask our grandmother if I had worn it. Even though she knew the truth, she always told him that it was probably dirty and in the hamper. She always does all she can to make my life a little easier.

Ever since she began living with us, I have tried my best to return her kindness. Just recently, for Mother's Day, I planned to buy her a pair of finches (tiny birds) that she had said she wanted. She wasn't expecting a present from me. But I had just started working on weekends and was getting paid well enough to buy her something special.

I left the house, telling everybody that I was going to the store. My grandmother was the only one who didn't know what I was up to. When I came back and gave her the finches, a great big smile was practically all I could see of her face. She kissed me as I said, *"Feliz día de madres"* ("Happy Mother's Day") to her. I felt so happy because I'd made her happy.

Daniel was 17 when he wrote this story.

D Alen Michailov

What I Learned From Roberto Clemente

By Luis Reyes

When I was 12 years old, I played for a baseball team called Puerto Rico. And what a hard and unhappy season I had.

I had practiced very hard, and at first I was hot. In my first five games, I hit six home runs and 14 RBIs (runs batted in). Everyone thought that we were going to be a championship team.

But after the 5th game, I went into a terrible slump. In the next four games, I was one for 16. And in one game, I dropped an easy pop up that made us lose.

After that game, no one wanted to speak to me. The team was so mad that I got into a fight with one of my own teammates, who told me that I should go try out for Little League. All those little words really hurt my feelings. And to make life worse, I was benched for the rest of the season.

I was bristling. But in some ways, it was good that I was benched because I was too scared to go back out and play. I had lost all faith in myself.

One day after I argued with our pitcher, my coach told me to sit down and relax. Then he started telling me that I reminded him of a baseball legend named Roberto Clemente.

"Who's Roberto Clemente?" I asked.

My coach told me that he was the first Puerto Rican star in the Major Leagues. He told me that there was a time when, like Jackie Robinson, Clemente was hated because of his race. But Clemente did not give up. My coach told me that Roberto Clemente was a man of heart.

After my coach told me this story, I decided to fish for more information. I went to the library and asked for old newspapers about his life and how he died.

I learned that, starting in the 1950s, Clemente played for the Pittsburgh Pirates for 15 seasons and helped lead them to two World Series. He also played in nine All-Star games, won the Most Valuable Player Award (MVP), four batting titles and 10 consecutive Gold Gloves. Amazing!

Learning about Roberto Clemente made me believe that if I work hard now, I can be somebody. I haven't always believed that.

On September 30, 1972, Clemente made his 3,000th career hit. Only 10 other players before him had made as many hits.

But his achievements came to a sudden end. On December 31, 1972, Clemente was killed in a plane crash while taking supplies to earthquake victims in Nicaragua.

In 1973, Clemente became the first Puerto Rican player to be admitted to the Baseball Hall of Fame. When I talked to my father, he told me that Clemente was always the first player on the field to practice. He said that when Clemente was down he always found a way to come up.

Learning about Roberto Clemente made me believe that if I

work hard now, I can be somebody. Knowing about Clemente made me see that Latino children could be as successful as any white, Chinese or black person on this planet.

I haven't always believed that. The people around me aren't very successful. Besides, there haven't been that many people in my life who have supported me, and lots of people put me down.

My sister was the only person who did encourage me—she helped me with my homework, hugged me when I cried, and told me, "Luis, I believe in you." But she died from drugs that summer when I was 12.

Before I learned about Clemente, I felt embarrassed about being Puerto Rican because a lot of the Latinos I hang out with are not good influences. Half of my friends want to succeed and want an education. They're trying their best to do well in their classes and prepare for the future. But the other half are either in gangs, in jail, on the streets or on their deathbeds.

Take my former friend, Edward, who is 18 years old and thinks he's all that. He's a high school dropout, but when I talked to him about changing his life around, he didn't want to hear it. Another friend, Jose, dropped out of high school in 10th grade and joined a gang. He told me he joined to help keep young Latinos from being pushed around.

I don't have anything against that. I just think that he should go back to school so he can help Latino children with his mind and heart, not with knives, guns and violence.

Sometimes I've almost slipped into the same rut my friends are in. Luckily, I've had positive teachers who actually cared for me. Still, all the teachers who have influenced me are black. Learning about Clemente made me realize that there are also Latinos out there who can be role models.

It also made me believe that my sister's spirit was still in me, and it gave me the strength to go outside with my friends every other day and run around the bases about 10 times. It gave me the will power to throw the ball from left field to home plate over and over. And it gave me the heart to stay outside and hit fast-balls that my neighborhood friends would throw me.

Today many younger people don't know about Clemente. But I think they should, because I bet anyone that if Roberto Clemente were alive today, young Latinos would not give up so quickly.

Clemente is my role model. If I had never learned about him, I would have given up a long time ago. It's because of him that I try to play with faith, confidence, power, and belief. That's why in 1996, I had a much better season, and I won my league's World Series MVP.

Roberto Clemente made me believe that it's not the way you begin that counts, it's the way you finish. And my team and I finished number one in a powerful way.

Luis was 15 when he wrote this story.

The Young Lords:
Rebels with a Cause

By David Miranda

When I think about all the homelessness in the streets, the poverty, the drug use, the way poor people get treated worse than people who have money—the list goes on and on—it makes me wonder why no one seems to really care. Everybody is always talking about how racist society is, or how we have a double system of justice, but is anybody really doing anything about it?

One group that did was the Young Lords Party, an organization of Puerto Rican youth who actually went out and did things to help their communities in the late '60s and early '70s. The Young Lords started out as a gang in Chicago. Then they came in contact with the Black Panthers, a group of militant black revolutionaries. Former Young Lord Ritchie Pérez says that the Panthers taught them that, "Instead of fighting each other we should be fighting the people hurting our community."

Their first big fight was with the New York City Sanitation Department. In 1969, poor communities (which are often the most crowded) were getting less garbage pickup services than the richer neighborhoods just a few blocks away.

The Young Lords started to clean up the streets of El Barrio in East Harlem. They went out on Sundays and swept up garbage and piled it on the corners so that the sanitation department could come and haul it away. "Look, we're gonna help you out," they told the city. "We're gonna sweep the streets and pile it up so that you could pick it up."

But the Sanitation Department wouldn't do their part and the Young Lords figured that unless they did something more drastic the garbage wasn't going anywhere. They took the garbage and put it in the middle of 1st and 2nd Avenues and burned it. That stopped traffic and attracted attention to their cause. The Sanitation Department finally did come and pick up the garbage. In fact, they picked up the garbage for months afterwards. "Unless you push against the system they never pay attention to you," explained Pérez.

The Young Lords believed that the system was killing their people, and they decided to do something about it.

The Young Lords believed that the system was killing their people with bad hospitals, lousy schools and unhealthy living conditions, and they decided to do something about it. When they saw that little kids often went to school hungry because they couldn't afford to eat breakfast, they started their own breakfast program.

"It wasn't easy to get up early in the morning to pick up the kids, walk them to school, and then feed them," said Pérez. "It took a lot of commitment...[but] we believed it was our responsibility to serve and protect our community."

The Lords also organized clothing drives, and pushed for

bilingual education, which didn't exist at the time, and for free, better health care for all people.

In 1970 the Young Lords set up tables in the lobby of Lincoln Hospital in the South Bronx and let people voice their complaints. They wrote down what they heard and sent it over to the hospital administrators, but got no response. So they took over the building, determined to give it back to the people. One of the things they wanted to do was start offering a drug treatment program. Fifteen percent of the population in the area that Lincoln Hospital served was addicted to heroin at that time, but there were no services for them.

"People would come in with heart attacks, cuts, shock, whatever it was, and they'd die sometimes waiting in the emergency room," writes Gloria Gonzales in the Young Lords' book, *Pa'lante*. "We decided it was time to move...About 100 people went to Lincoln and we took it over. We had gotten the support of the workers and the patients at Lincoln. At times we'd even have to stop some patients from just grabbing some doctor's throat, 'cause the patients had just had it with this hospital.

"While we were there we wanted to set up preventative programs, a day care program, do anemia testing, TB testing, lead poisoning screening—all those programs that [were] not being done in the municipal hospitals. But we were only there for 24 hours, a little less...before we knew it the place was surrounded by police and we had to leave."

The system also made people of color believe that they had no history. Through the media they got the idea that they were criminals and would amount to nothing (sound familiar?). So the Young Lords set up "Liberation Schools" and ran classes to teach people Puerto Rican history. For a lot of the members it was the first time they ever learned about their own history.

"The best thing about being in the group was learning to be proud to be Puerto Rican," said Pérez, "learning about our people's history and contributions and the things that were done against us. I think that the Young Lords greatest contribution is that we made people proud to be Puerto Rican."

Mark Torres, a member of Fuerza Latina, a group of young people that is modeled after the Young Lords, said he was inspired by their boldness. "They were willing to do things that other so-called leaders weren't willing to do," he said. "It took a lot of love and commitment for them to put their lives on the line for our people."

But the Young Lords had a lot of problems within the organization which, according to Pérez, eventually pulled them apart.

At that time the FBI had a program called COINTELPRO to break up militant groups like the Young Lords and Black Panthers from the inside. The FBI would put an undercover agent in the group to encourage conflict and suspicion and instigate fights among the members. Some people in the Black Panthers even killed each other. Pérez says the Young Lords were also a target of the FBI's program.

Most of the Young Lords were the children of immigrants and they were almost all teenagers—some as young as 14.

People often want other people to do for them what they should be doing themselves. The Young Lords were regular people just like you and me. Most of them were the children of immigrants and they were almost all teenagers—some as young as 14. The majority were poor and lived in ghettos like the South Bronx, or in El Barrio or the Lower East Side in Manhattan. Some were high school dropouts, others were college educated, but they all had one thing in common: they decided to stop talking and take action.

So next time you say, "Damn, I'm sick of seeing all these homeless people on the street," or "I hate the fact that in my neighborhood the streets are dirty," ask yourself what you plan to do about it. Are you just going to let it happen, or will you volunteer at a homeless shelter or organize a cleanup on your block? It's up to you. You can either be part of the problem or part of the solution.

"Learn from the past," advises Pérez. "Understand that you are the continuation of this history. Ten years from now what you do today will be the history we study."

David was 17 when he wrote this story.

Sheila Maldonado

Los Buitres, Roadblocks, and Mayan Ruins

By Sheila Maldonado

Two years ago, my half-brother Waldo talked me into spending the summer with him in Honduras, the country my family is from. It is an extremely poor country in Central America, near Nicaragua and El Salvador.

I'd been there a few times before, always with my mother. When I was 2, I went there and almost died of dysentery, a painful stomach infection that causes fever and severe diarrhea. You get it from drinking contaminated water or eating unclean food. Because conditions were so bad in Honduras, thousands of babies died of diarrhea every year.

I remembered a hot, boring place where the mosquitoes tore you to pieces and the food and water made you sick.

My brother assured me if I stayed with his side of the family that summer, I wouldn't have to go through all that. He painted a picture of blue seas, white sand beaches, kids my own age (15), and memories that would last a lifetime. It would be my first time away from my mother for any real period of time. I was scared but I agreed to go.

After a 10-hour flight, the plane came down over muddy rivers and miles and miles of coconut and banana palm trees all arranged in neat rows.

Inside the little airport, soldiers stood around in dark glasses, fatigues, and combat boots. Over their shoulders were slung machine guns. At the time of my visit, Honduras was almost completely controlled by the military (and the United States), even though it had a president and a congress. We saw soldiers everywhere we went, and they weren't exactly friendly.

As we lined up to go through customs, we were praying the officials wouldn't take a liking to any of the gifts we were bringing for the family. They didn't.

The flight and the heat and the soldiers were taking their toll and I just wanted to get wherever we were going. I was glad that Waldo's aunt and uncle picked us up at the airport.

Along the road was a military checkpoint where everyone had to stop. Some officers had been found killed a few days earlier and the government was accusing the communists. They set up "*retenes*" (roadblocks) all over the area and were searching for anything suspicious. They examined our passports and went through all our luggage.

One of them, a man in his 50s with a beer belly and a slow cowboy walk (they all seemed to have that walk) accused me of coming to Honduras to sell the clothes in my suitcases. (That would have been illegal.) He was just trying to scare a little kid and he stopped bothering me after Waldo explained to him that I had just overpacked. To a 15-year-old in a foreign country without her mother, it was all pretty scary.

When we finally got to the house in San Pedro, I went to bed early and cried myself to sleep, wishing I was back in Coney Island, my neighborhood in Brooklyn, New York.

The town where we stayed had everything from little wooden shacks to huge, flashy mansions with big metal fences around them and four-by-fours in the driveways. The group of teenagers my brother hung out with was called *los buitres* (the vultures). They'd sit on a little bridge by the corner and yell rude comments whenever some girl in a miniskirt passed by.

Los buitres were famous for their mischief. The religious old ladies used to call them lazy bums and *marijuaneros* (potheads). Once they fixed it so some of these ladies got locked in the church courtyard and someone had to call a blacksmith to pry the gate open.

Another time the school band was marching through the streets at 5 a.m. practicing for the Independence Day parade. *Los buitres* silenced them with flying bags of urine.

Every once in a while you'd see *los buitres* suddenly scatter in all directions. That was because they had spotted the infamous yellow Datsun of the military police. It wasn't that they had done anything wrong. In Honduras all young men were required to do two years of military service. Kids as young as 14 and 15 could be picked up off the street and put in the army.

Watching out for the "DIN" (Department of National Investigation) was second nature to these guys. It got so they could even smell the car's diesel engine a few blocks away. A couple of them had been caught and came back with stories of being beaten up, made to strip down to their underwear and being thrown into a cell with bums and drunks.

Scary as it sounds, this stuff became the raw material for their jokes and insults. I guess it helped them maintain their sanity and mask their anger. It was better for them not to hold a grudge, especially against the men in uniforms.

My first few days there dragged on forever. I was surrounded by strangers. There was nothing to do and the heat was driving me insane. I kept telling my brother I wanted to go home.

Waldo was the only one I could really talk to. I spoke Spanish, but not really well, and I didn't want to make a bad impression or make a fool of myself.

One Sunday a neighbor offered to take us to Copán, an ancient ruined city. The three adults got in the front seat of his pick-up truck and the rest of us hopped in the back. We traveled up out of the valley and into the Honduran mountains. The road started turning sharply and we had to hold on for dear life as we stood in the back of the truck.

All around us there was nothing but sky and greenery, and we screamed every time we imagined we had another brush with death. We yelled and laughed through the strong and silencing wind. We whistled at men in approaching cars, flirted with people on passing busses, and made jokes about the people by the roadside. Sometimes we just

A soldier with a slow cowboy walk accused me of coming to Honduras to sell the clothes in my suitcases.

stared at the deep green and never-ending scenery. It was the longest, most exciting roller coaster ride I've ever taken (and I grew up in Coney Island, home of the famous Cyclone roller coaster).

Copán was a major city of the Mayas, the native people who lived in Southern Mexico, Guatemala, and Honduras in the times before Columbus came to America.

The Mayas, like the Incas of Peru and the ancient Greeks and Egyptians, were one of the most advanced civilizations ever.

The ruins were a massive complex of stone temples, pyramids, sculptures and wide-open spaces. There were huge slabs of rough, beige rock (called steles) more than twice my height and the surfaces were carved with images of elaborately dressed Mayan rulers. They were worn down by time and weather but were still powerful to look at.

We started exploring the temples. I couldn't believe all

this took up only two pages in my history textbook. We climbed up the steps and got a perfect view of the whole place. Archaeologists were still digging a lot of it up. There were stones all over the place. Some of them had carvings of skulls and the faces of Mayan gods.

We saw a gigantic tree, hundreds of years old with the soil on one side cut away so you could see the roots. They were wrapped around a big slab of rock covered with hieroglyphic writing. It looked as if the tree had sprouted from a giant writing tablet.

Then we realized that the hieroglyphic slab was just a part of something much larger. Underneath the hill we were standing on was buried an entire temple.

We discovered a series of interconnecting tunnels through which the Mayas could escape if the city was being invaded. With no one around to tell us not to, we decided to explore one for ourselves. My brother went first.

We were all pretty small and still could barely squeeze through the entrance. Inside it was dark and damp, almost slimy. There wasn't a lot of air and we were all getting short of breath.

My brother almost hit his head on a piece of rock hanging down from the ceiling. He stopped for a second and felt the rock, then stuck his foot out to take another step. There was nothing, no place to step, just a dark, gaping hole. We got out of there as fast as we could. We were all pretty spooked.

On the way back home we stopped in the town of Copán Ruinas to get something to drink. This place was right out of a fairy tale: gleaming cobblestone streets and a bright, white Spanish church on the plaza.

My brother and I were sitting outside drinking our sodas when two small, thin, barefoot girls came over selling souvenirs. They were wearing dingy little dresses and their hair was a mess but they were both incredibly beautiful. The older of the two was no more than 10 or 11. Her name was Esmeralda, Spanish for emerald, the color of her eyes.

Esmeralda was nothing like those third-world kids they ask you to sponsor on TV. She didn't seem sad or lost; she was vibrant and proud. She told us she and her sister walked four miles every day to sell souvenirs and help support their family.

She asked us questions about who we were and where we were from. The way she spoke was confident and adult-like. She had wit and plenty of charm and seemed to know it. All the time, Esmeralda was making a sale.

Kids like her have to grow up fast. They have to learn to carry themselves as adults in order to survive. I didn't pity Esmeralda like I did the children in those commercials—she made me respect her. In the end she gave us one of the little Mayan stone blocks she was selling, but we still paid her twice what it was worth.

After we got back to San Pedro I wasn't afraid to talk to people anymore. I became less self-conscious about my Spanish and once I loosened up it just seemed to flow from my lips. My brother's cousins and I would gossip about the boys in the neighborhood, watch *telenovelas* (soap operas) and go to the movies. I did their English homework for them and they taught me how to dance the punta and the merengue. We found our own little bridge to hang out on and sang Spanish pop songs at the top of our lungs.

The four weeks I was supposed to stay in Honduras turned into six. When I got back to New York my parents didn't even recognize me. I had gotten thinner and darker and even started to look more Honduran. And they were stunned by the Spanish that gushed out of me.

Of course six weeks isn't enough time to really find out what it's like to live in another country. But at least I got my taste.

Sheila was 17 when she wrote this story. She later graduated from Brown University.

Michael Aurello

Leaving '*El Combito*'

By Angy Gonzalez

The day I left Colombia for the United States, I was thinking every second about my friends. I hadn't said goodbye to them. I couldn't bear to.

Standing in the airport at age 12, it was as if I had a photo of *el combito* (that's what my friends and I called ourselves) in my empty hand. A picture of a bunch of noisy kids growing together, not only physically but mentally—experimenting with new things together, watching one another's backs, covering one another's mistakes, talking to one another like family.

I saw myself vanishing from that picture, and then gone. I felt such a deep sadness that day. Even if I were leaving today, almost five years later, I don't think I could say goodbye.

My *combito* were my friends during 6th and part of 7th grade. We had all our classes together and were always talking and making jokes during class. Maribel, who looked older than the rest of us, was my closest friend. Pilar was short but very aggressive and Angelica was a starter in basketball. Fernanda was the youngest and Paola was the friendly but sad one. Last but not least was me, the sweet but noisy girl.

We came up with thousands of lame names for our group, like "white witches" and "mean freshmen" (*las odiosas primiparas*). But we stuck with *"el combito."* We used to eat all the junky food we could afford, and we'd always order the combo meal (*el combito*), which had six things: soda, French fries, a hamburger, a hot dog, special salsa and dessert.

Since we were initially a group of six girls who fit together like the combo, we started calling ourselves *el combito*. Separately, we were six unique girls, but together we formed a magic and rare flavor. In the middle of 6th grade Diana became the seventh girl to join us. Later, guys started joining too—Freddie, a metal fan, and Francisco, the cutest guy at school.

You can have as many acquaintances as you can count. But real friends you can count within your two hands.

We played basketball at lunchtime and sometimes cut class and went behind some old buildings. There was a big green yard near a basketball court where we drank, cried, smoked and gossiped.

This was my first time in public school. I think I became especially close to my new friends because they seemed more real than my old private school friends, most of whom were wealthy and never had to work for anything. My new friends opened me up to a world richer in trust and understanding. We listened to and supported one another.

Maribel helped me realize it was better for me to stay with my mom instead of moving in with my father and stepmother. When Angelica and Diana talked about how badly their fathers treated them, Francisco encouraged them to break free from their abusive homes.

Freddie shared his dreams of someday going to college and traveling to other continents. And when Paola didn't have enough money for lunch or simply to get to school, we pooled our money to help her.

I felt so peaceful and secure to have friends who cared about my feelings and gave me advice. Nowadays I have friends who kind of listen, but most of the time I feel I'm the one giving advice instead of receiving it.

El combito taught me the meaning of real friendship—having people you can truly trust, who care about you and won't spread your secrets around, and who are always there, even when they're not physically present. You can have as many acquaintances as you can count. But real friends you can count within your two hands.

The first time I told *el combito* I was leaving, they thought it was only for vacation. Later I told them, "I'm moving forever." When my mom decided to move to the U.S., I chose to go with her rather than live in Colombia with my father, who didn't feel like my father anymore because he didn't seem to care about my life.

My friends were happy for me, since in Colombia the U.S. seems like the land of opportunity. But then Maribel started crying and said, "Now who am I going to talk to?" That made me feel like the worst friend in the world.

"So, when are you leaving exactly?" Freddie asked.

"I don't know, I think our flight is next month," I said.

They started making plans to go to the airport with me. They were all talking at once, as usual. "We're going to be there at the airport singing our song for you," they said. It was a song we'd composed describing how we'd gotten together and who we were. The title was *"El Combo, No Una Pandilla"* (The Combo, Not a Gang).

I started crying and begged them, "Please, if you love me, don't come to the airport!" They were shocked to see me crying so hard. Maribel continued crying along with me.

I explained that seeing them in the airport would make it even worse. Just the idea of not seeing them again was enough to make me cry harder. I'd never graduate with them, go to the prom or on the senior trip.

They changed the subject and then Francisco said, "You see, we never hooked up and now you're leaving me!" Everyone broke into laughter, since he wasn't the kind of guy who expressed his feelings openly.

My face turned red as an apple, my legs started shaking and my heart felt like it was coming out of my chest. I'd always had a crush on Francisco but never knew he had feelings for me until that moment. I was in heaven knowing he felt the same way I did.

Francisco touched my face with his soft hand and gave me a warm hug. Even though I was leaving, he told me I should give him a chance. "I don't want to wonder what would've happened if we'd gone out. I know you're going to leave me, but it's better to have a memory with you than just an illusion," he said.

I begged them, "Please, if you love me, don't come to the airport!" Just the idea of not seeing them again was enough to make me cry harder.

Those words broke my heart even more. After that, Francisco became my first real boyfriend. I will always remember him as the sweetest Colombian guy I ever met.

My last day of school, in the middle of 7th grade, another friend from school, Sandra, started writing on my white school shirt. She drew a funny girl that looked exactly like her and wrote, "Don't forget about me, girl, and what we went through. You know you're crazy but I love you anyway."

All of a sudden everyone at school was writing on me. They didn't even ask—it was like, grab a pen and write on Angy. Some people I didn't even know were saying good luck and were happy for me. My classmate Carolina wrote, "Now you're going to be the gringa (white girl) you always looked like."

I walked through the school wearing that shirt, and I never opened my mouth to say goodbye. I tried hard not to cry, so that they'd remember me as they'd always known me—with a big, happy smile.

After school I met up with *el combito*. They were all making jokes and playing around. I stood there with my written-on shirt, some love letters I'd received, a bracelet from Maribel and a big hug from *el combito*. There are no words to describe how vulnerable I felt. It was the last time I saw them.

For a while after I moved here, I spoke to Maribel on the phone a lot, but then she moved and I lost touch with her. The last she told me was that *el combito* had broken apart.

Pilar dropped out of school. Fernanda, Angelica, Diana, Paola, Freddie and Francisco continued being friends but weren't as close as we all once were. Maribel also said that Francisco didn't go out with anyone for almost a year after I left.

I painfully regret not saying goodbye. But I knew if I saw them the day I left, I wouldn't be able to get on the plane, and I'd be living miserably there now with my father.

So instead I left quietly, with only the memory of my friends to help me as I struggled to learn to be myself once again, this time in an American world.

Angy was 17 when she wrote this story.

Karolina Zaniesienko

Torn Between Two Countries

By Anghela Calvo

I think I had a beautiful childhood. I lived in La Paz, Bolivia, with my grandparents (my father's parents) and my Aunt Lucy. We lived in a quiet neighborhood where we knew everyone.

When I was 2, my parents left Bolivia looking for a better life in the United States. They couldn't take me because both of them had to work.

But my grandparents always gave me love. And Aunt Lucy was like a mother to me. She spent most of her free time with me. She gave me toys, took me to the park and played with dolls with me. I was very attached to her.

I still loved and missed my parents, but they were so far away and had left when I was so young that I didn't know them very well. I just had pictures of them, and of my little brother and sister who were born in America. When I looked at the pictures,

I wanted to be with them as a family.

My dad called me every weekend. One week before I turned 9, he asked me if I wanted to go to New York and live with them. "Of course!" I answered, not thinking twice.

I thought it would be exciting to live in New York City, full of big skyscrapers and snow in the winter. I was excited to meet my siblings. But I couldn't imagine living with my parents again because I didn't remember how it was to be with them.

Then one day my father arrived at our house with my mom and my siblings, ages 2 and 3. I was so happy to meet them. Suddenly I was a big sister and no longer the youngest in my house. I felt responsible for them and made sure I was always with them.

Everything was different here. The streets were bigger and the food tasted like medicine.

They stayed a few weeks, and from the moment they left, I was crossing off the days on the calendar, waiting to join them in New York. But as the day of my trip got closer, I started to worry about my grandparents. I thought that I might not see them again. Would I ever come back? And what was going to happen to Aunt Lucy? I was like the daughter she never had and I worried she'd suffer without me.

I was also afraid of starting a new life in a strange place where everyone spoke a different language.

When the day of my trip came, I was nervous. By the time I reached the airport with my family and friends, I didn't want to go, and I told my aunt.

"You have to go. Everything is ready," she said. "But if you don't like living there, you could always come back. We'd be waiting for you."

When I entered the plane I was crying, my grandparents were crying, my aunt was crying, even my friends were crying.

One the plane, the dinner was different from the food I was used to eating. It was pasta with chicken and a white sauce and it didn't taste like anything. I couldn't make myself eat it. In my country, I was used to spicy food with different condiments.

"Is everything going to taste like that in the U.S.?" I wondered. I felt sad again and I remembered all the special moments with my grandparents, like when my grandfather taught me how to draw, and when my grandmother made dinner and I helped her. I started crying, and while I cried I fell asleep.

My father met me in Miami. I hugged him like he was saving me from a monster. He asked me how the trip was and I answered, "Fine," even though I'd spent most of the flight crying.

While we waited for the flight to New York, we ate pizza, which I was happy to eat because in Bolivia I ate a lot of pizza. Then we bought T-shirts and souvenirs. It was fun spending time alone with my dad.

When we flew into New York, the view of the city was wonderful. The city's lights were like shining gold. It was like discovering a treasure.

At the airport, I was excited because my uncles, aunts and cousins had come to see me. But I was still missing my grandparents and Aunt Lucy.

Everything was different here. The streets were bigger and I saw people from various countries wearing different clothes. The food tasted like medicine. Even the milk tasted odd to me. I felt like a stranger.

But my family made me feel welcome. I shared a room with my siblings and I loved playing with them. We had a connection even though we'd never lived together. As a full-time big sister, I also had to be more responsible and help my siblings do their homework and get dressed for school.

My parents were glad to have me with them. They used me as an example for my siblings, so my little sister was always trying to be like me.

School, though, made me feel unwelcome. My father registered me at the public school nearby. I'd finished 5th grade in

Bolivia, where I'd gone to an all-girls school, but the principal here placed me in the bilingual class for 4th graders because there was none for 5th graders.

I felt uncomfortable because I knew all the things they were learning except English.

And some girls from my class were mean to me at lunch and during free periods. My first week at school, they took my lunch tray from the table and ate my lunch. After that, I just sat alone at a table without eating anything, or asked my mom if she could make lunch for me. That way I could eat in the auditorium instead of the cafeteria.

I felt pressured by everything—my aunt on one side, my father on the other. Whichever choice I made would upset someone.

Between the problems at school and missing my family in Bolivia, I regretted coming to New York. "I should have stayed in Bolivia," I said to myself every night as I cried alone after my siblings fell asleep. I wished I could disappear from New York and appear in Bolivia.

I usually told my parents that everything in school was OK because I didn't want them to worry about me. But after two months of keeping my discomfort a secret, my feelings came out. One day I felt so bad, I started crying while we were eating dinner.

"Why are you crying?" my father asked.

"I hate school! I want to go back to Bolivia," I said. I couldn't stop crying and my little sister stared at me.

"But tell me your problem. I'm sure we can find a solution," my dad said, worried.

"I don't like how my classmates treat me. Can the principal change me to another class?" I asked my dad.

"I'll talk to him tomorrow," he said.

My father talked to the principal and the next week I joined the 5th grade, which meant I had a different lunch period too. Soon I was learning new things and improving my English more than in the bilingual class. I met two Mexican girls who were kind to me and I started hanging around with them.

But the other kids were pretty much the same as the kids in my last class. They made fun of my clothes, telling me that I dressed like a little girl. I ignored their comments, but they hurt my feelings.

So I still hated school, and I missed my grandparents and aunt. I didn't want to talk with them on the phone because I missed them more when I heard their voices. I just wrote them letters telling them I was OK, but that things would be better if I had them with me.

After I'd been here a year, my grandfather called my dad and invited us to Aunt Lucy's wedding. I couldn't believe she was getting married. I was jealous because I thought she'd have her own kids and wouldn't love me anymore.

I asked my dad if I could go with him to Bolivia for the wedding. He agreed but made me promise that I'd come back to New York with him.

At the time, I never thought I'd stay in Bolivia. I knew what I promised my father was important. But I wondered how life would be if I did stay.

One week later, I went back to Bolivia with my Aunt Lourdes; my father planned to join us later. I was excited to see my grandparents and especially Aunt Lucy.

When I arrived at my old house, almost everything was just how I left it, except that my old room on the second floor was dark and empty. Now I had a bigger and nicer room, which my aunt prepared with all the things from my old room, plus a new TV. I was surprised. I felt like everything was in place for me to stay.

That day, Aunt Lucy, her fiancé and I went to the movies and to eat burgers. When we got back, my aunt said she wanted to talk to me. We sat on my bed, and she told me how much she missed me. She asked me to stay and live with them again.

I was very confused. I told her I had to think about my decision carefully. I had to weigh the good and the bad things about staying.

"I'd never see those annoying girls anymore," I thought. "But I'd miss my family in the U.S." I had so many bad experiences in the U.S. but I was overcoming those obstacles day by day. What was I going to do?

I felt pressured by everything—my aunt on one side, my father on the other. Whichever choice I made would upset someone. I had to figure out what was best for me.

I decided to stay in Bolivia.

After a week, my father arrived. I was terrified to tell him because my father was very strict and I was scared of his reaction.

Two days later, while he was watching TV, I approached him and told him what I wanted to do. He was shocked and reminded me of my promise. But I told him I wanted to stay with my grandparents and my aunt because I missed them so much. He wasn't angry but he looked disappointed.

I had so many bad experiences in the U.S. but I was overcoming those obstacles day by day. What was I going to do?

"If you want to stay, you can. But I don't accept that idea," he told me. I felt so bad because I loved him, but I wanted to stay.

I stayed and he left, alone. He called me when he arrived and told me that my siblings were very sad because I hadn't arrived with him and they were waiting for me. I felt so bad, because they were so attached to me and I left them. But I didn't regret my decision because I was happy living in Bolivia.

I stayed with my grandparents, my aunt and her new husband. There were bad moments. My aunt separated from her husband after three years. My grandmother died when I was 13. Her death affected my grandfather's health, and he needed to move to a city that wasn't as cold as La Paz. We ended up moving a few times.

I visited my parents every two years, staying for one month. But I didn't plan to stay in New York because even with all the hardships, I preferred my life in Bolivia.

I don't regret what I did because I wasn't happy with the life I had in New York and I felt that I wasn't prepared enough for the big change. But after five years, when I was 15, I wanted to try adapting to New York again. Now that I'd moved a few times, it was not the big deal it once was for me. I also thought that going to college in the U.S. would be better for my future. So I came back to New York.

I miss my grandfather and friends in Boliva, but at least this time Aunt Lucy came with me. I don't know how long I'll stay here, or whether I'll choose to stay or go back to Boliva. But I do know it will be my own decision.

Anghela was 16 when she wrote this story.

See Anghela's story about learning to love Bolivian culture, starting on the next page.

Gary Smith

Learning to Love
My Bolivian Culture

By Anghela Calvo

La Paz, the city where I spent most of my childhood, is the most modern city in Bolivia. It has tall buildings and busy highways, and its narrow streets are crowded with commercial stores and business people.

People in La Paz tend to value things from outside the country over native Bolivian things. They imitate the music, culture and image of foreign countries, particularly America and Europe. For example, some teen girls dye their hair light blonde and use green or blue contact lenses because they want to be like Britney Spears or Christina Aguilera.

Bolivia has its own music tradition, but many people in La Paz believe the music of our country is for town people and peasants. They'd only listen to that music for the August 6

Independence Day parade or in a folklore festival.

Growing up in La Paz, I used to think that too. My grandparents listened to folklore music. I thought that was fine for them, but not for me. When I was 13, I didn't listen to anything but pop music in English. I didn't even listen to music in Spanish.

I also didn't like wearing traditional costumes in plays or dances. I felt embarrassed in front of my friends. We thought that wearing those clothes was for peasants; we were modern. I preferred to dress like the teenagers I saw in TV shows or in teen magazines. I felt cool doing these things.

When I was 14, my family moved to Tarija, a city at the other end of Bolivia. I didn't like the idea at all. Tarija's one of the smallest cities in Bolivia and I thought it was going to be boring.

Fortunately, though, when I started 11th grade in Tarija, I met two girls, Adriana and Lizeth, who were very nice to me. It was fun hanging around with them. We'd go often to movies after they'd started so we could get in for half-price.

One day while we were listening to the radio at Lizeth's house, the station started playing a folklore song. I was shocked. I couldn't believe they were playing that kind of music; that station usually played pop in Spanish. I was just about to say, "What the hell is that music?" when I heard both of them singing along. They knew all the lyrics.

I didn't understand why they liked it. Listening to that irritating music was torture for me. It had the same melody over and over again and without electric instruments or special sounds — just acoustic guitar, some violin and drums. It sounded so simple. I dismissed it as rustic, country music.

The song brought back bad memories of a dance I had to do in 4th grade. I was in an all-girls school and I had to dress like a boy and dance the boy's role, which I hated doing.

When the song finished, they started talking about all the other groups and singers that performed folklore. Then Adriana asked Lizeth if she had the latest CD by folklore singer Juan Enrique Jurado. Lizeth put on the CD and they knew practically all the songs.

I thought they were crazy. How could they be the same age as me and listen to that music? They should be listening to pop or rock, or even tropical music, but not that!

I thought that maybe my new friends spent too much time with their grandparents and that was the reason they liked that music. But Lizeth and Adriana were not the only ones. I soon discovered that my other classmates liked folklore music too. When we gathered together to study or hang out, they put on folklore music. I stared at them like they were crazy.

A few weeks later, my grandfather arrived home very happy because he'd bought a new CD.

"Do you wanna listen to it?" he asked me.

"Why not," I replied. I thought it was going to be classical music, like most of his CDs. But to my surprise, this CD was similar to the one Lizeth had. It was like this music was following me and no matter how I tried to escape it, I couldn't.

But I listened to it with my grandfather and this time I found something interesting about the songs. They had very poetic lyrics. The singer, Negro Palma, wrote his own songs, expressing the beauty of rivers surrounded by mountains and valleys in the Chaco region, where he's from.

In every song, he expressed the love he had for his Bolivia. The frequent violins gave the songs a sweet sound like a cricket's "cri-cri." I asked my grandfather to lend me his CD and soon I started borrowing Lizeth's and Adriana's folklore music.

People in the little city of Tarija had less exposure to American and European culture, and they considered it normal to embrace traditional Bolivian culture. My classmates enjoyed many country traditions. They'd rather go on a picnic than to a mall. They preferred the beauty of a river to an artificial pool.

And I started to embrace traditional Bolivian culture too. I began to feel that this music was a part of me.

I watched TV shows of festivals and videos of people dancing to folklore music. I wanted to be like the dancers. The girls looked like butterflies when they spread out their wide colorful dresses by grasping the bottom in their hands. And the boys wore black hats and boots that made a tap-tap-tap when their heels touched the ground.

When I went to my friend's prom, I tried to dance to the folklore songs they played toward the end of the party but I looked like a housefly instead of a butterfly. My other friends didn't know much either, but I saw many couples dancing perfectly. That day I decided that I'd learn how to dance to folklore music. I didn't want to look like an oaf at the next party I'd go to.

I was just about to say, "What the hell is that music?" when I heard both of my friends singing along. They knew all the lyrics.

I entered a dance academy where I learned the basic steps of each dance. I learned how to identify each dance by the different instruments used. For example, songs with violin at the beginning last longer than songs without the violin.

At the beginning it was difficult, especially the boy's role, because you need to have balance with your feet to do the tap-tap-tap. The boy's role is harder than the girl's, but I wanted to learn both.

After two weeks of practicing hard at the academy, I felt prepared. I couldn't wait to show what I'd learned. The next party was my grandfather's birthday.

To surprise him, my mom and my aunt found a group to play for the party. They were excellent, and their clothes and instruments were covered with colorful wool in the traditional style. When they started performing, the first to dance with my grandpa was my aunt and then my mom.

Then it was my turn. I was so happy to dance with him and felt so good that this time I knew what I was doing. My grandfather's family and friends were impressed.

I learned a lot about myself when I discovered traditional Bolivian music and dance. It made me realize that Bolivia has an incredible variety of traditions and melodies.

I used to follow English-language music because I wanted to be cool. But now I'm happy I know more about my culture. Even though I live in New York now, I love Bolivia and I'm not ashamed of its music anymore. It represents my culture no matter where I am.

Anghela was 16 when she wrote this story.

Percyell Smith and YC Art Dept

Can I Have Both?

By Fanny Brito

"Look, this is a *platano*," said Enrique, an old classmate I ran into at a supermarket in the Dominican Republic last spring break. I'd moved to New York two years before, and this was my first time back.

"Umm...I know what a *platano* is. I happen to eat them all the time back in New York," I said, feeling offended. Still, it's not the first time I've been treated like a tourist in my own country.

When I'm in the Dominican Republic, I feel like I belong there. But other Dominicans see me differently because I've lived in America. Though it bothers me, I'm starting to realize that it's true: being American as well as Dominican makes me different.

Although I was born in New York, I've lived most of my life—about 11 of my 17 years—in the Dominican Republic. When I went back last April, I was anxious and happy to see my old friends and family. I got off the airplane and took slow steps, immediately closing my eyes to the shining sun. The moment I felt that familiar breeze of warm, humid air in my face, I knew I was home.

My parents have been dragging me back and forth between the two countries since I can remember. They'd spend one year working really hard in New York; then they'd move back to the Dominican Republic (DR) and try to make a living there by buying properties—like houses, cars and land—and renting them out.

I was happy when, in 4th grade, we moved back to the DR to stay for several years. I had my own bedroom instead of sharing a room with my parents like I did in New York. And I liked being able to go outside and play with my friends in our yard.

In New York, my parents worked long hours, but in the DR they were home much more, and I spent more time with them. Unlike in New York, we ate most meals together.

My relatives acted like I was different because I'd lived in the United States.

I liked having my mom with me. She taught me "chores every woman should know," like how to iron, cook and clean. My dad taught me how to wash his car and change the tires so that when I'm old enough to have my own car, I won't need any men to help me. (Though I think he just wanted somebody to wash his car for him.)

While I felt I was living a typical Dominican kid's life in a typical Dominican family, some of my relatives acted like I was different because I'd lived in the United States. At the time, I didn't understand it.

Occasionally some of my cousins would act as if I had nothing in common with them. They asked me questions to test my "Dominican abilities," like did I know how to cook, how to clean, iron or wash my clothes, things that are expected of girls my age in the DR, and the same things that my mother had taught me.

They were surprised to learn that I could do them, too.

Sometimes they'd go into one of the bedrooms and not invite me to go with them. I tried to ignore them, but I felt left out. They also acted very defensive around me as if I thought I was better than them, which I didn't.

Other people in the DR I'd known my whole life treated me like a tourist. They called me *gringa* or *la Americana*. My aunts and uncles referred to me, like they did to my parents, in a more formal way than the rest of their nieces and nephews. They'd use "*usted*" (the formal version of "you") rather than the more casual "*tu*."

I didn't feel like I deserved special treatment. And having them treat me that way somehow built a barrier between us. I wasn't able to joke around with them as I did with my other uncles and aunts back in New York.

I think they treated me this way because being "American" usually means you have more money, and with more money comes a higher social status. Many people said we were wealthy.

And it's true that even though we lived uncomfortably when we lived in New York, in the DR my family had a car and a nice house. It had three full-size bedrooms, each with a big closet; one bathroom; two dining rooms; a living room; a big kitchen; and two big galerias. (A galeria is like a screened-in porch, only with bars around it.) We had a backyard and front yard with mango, orange and lemon trees that my dad planted to remind himself of how he grew up, growing his own food.

That's more than most families have in the DR. Most of my relatives there don't have cars, and they have smaller houses in not-so-good neighborhoods. They have enough for their basic necessities and sometimes enough to go out to dinner or to the movies, but that's a luxury. Most of them work in textile factories and dress in a simple way, wearing inexpensive clothes.

But what my relatives and friends in the DR didn't see was my family's cramped lifestyle in New York and my parents' hard work and long hours.

Dominicans who've never come to New York only see the end results for the people who go to New York to work. They have no idea how hard it is for uneducated Dominican immigrants, who often work about 12 hours a day in a hot, unsafe factory in New York to make a lame amount of money.

My parents and many of my relatives worked this way when they first arrived. And because rent in New York is so expensive, "home" is often just a small bedroom in a relative's house.

People in the Dominican Republic who I'd known my whole life treated me like a tourist. They called me **gringa** *or* **la Americana.**

Every time my family moved back to New York, my parents would usually buy a grocery store and work about 12 hours a day, seven days a week.

In New York, we lived in a small apartment with my aunt, her husband, and her two teenage kids; my parents and I shared a small room. Most of the time, my mother and father were tired and cranky when they got home, complaining about things and fighting with me because I misbehaved or didn't clean my side of the room.

Still, living like that was worth it because making it in the Dominican Republic is hard. My parents used to tell me about how bad their circumstances were before they came to New York. They worked very hard in the DR, but they were only able to afford their everyday needs, never able to save money.

My father was in the DR army for a few years. He drove a truck, and then he and my mother managed to buy a grocery store there. They had to sell their house when they decided to come to the US the first time, to pay for the plane tickets and the paperwork. But working hard in the United States paid off for them. They saved money. When they came back to the DR, they could buy things.

At first, it's easy to feel rich coming back from New York to the DR. When you live and work only in the DR, things seem very expensive, the same as when you live and work in New York.

But when you work in New York and take dollars to the DR, things seem very cheap. For example, a haircut in a salon there cost me 60 pesos—about $3; in New York a haircut usually costs me $25.

My family is a vivid example of how hard work in New York can get you further than in the DR. But more than I want to admit, my family's hard work in New York has made me la Americana in some ways.

Now I realize I really am different from my relatives in the DR. As an American citizen, I have the opportunity to choose between the U.S. and the DR, unlike my relatives in the DR who have to stay there. And part of me feels more comfortable in the U.S.

When I was in 9th grade and we'd been living in the DR for five years straight, my parents decided we were moving back to New York. I was glad. My life in the DR had started to feel limited because young people there don't have the same expectations and opportunities I'd been raised with. Like many American families, my parents expect me to go to school, start a career and then form a family.

Although things are changing, young people in the DR are expected to marry and form a family when they are young (early 20s), and most women stay home and take care of the children. It's also difficult to go to college in the DR because it's extremely expensive and there's very little help with paying tuition. Only middle class people who live in cities are expected to go to college and have careers.

When I thought about what I want for my future, I realized how much I wanted something different from what my family has in the DR. I plan to finish my senior year of high school and then to college in the U.S. Like my parents, I see more opportunities here than in the DR. My future is in the U.S.

I'm glad that New York adopted us (and many other immigrants) and gives us many opportunities that we couldn't have in the DR. I love this city, its people, its controversies, its opportunities. But I also feel grateful that my parents raised me in two places.

Spending most of my childhood in the DR, I was able to learn my home country's values and culture. I like how people in the DR are friendly and funny, laid-back and not stressed.

In New York, you don't pass by a person's house and say hi to them if you don't know them, while in the DR, that's expected. There's life in the streets—people playing dominos, hanging out, talking. Days feel longer in the DR: You have time to visit people at their houses, to drink a cup of coffee while you're sitting down, something I've never done in New York.

Sometimes I really miss it.

Fanny was 17 when she wrote this story.

Rosheed Wellington

Lost in the Desert

By Pedro Cruz

I grew up with this dream: To arrive one day in the United States. As a poor teen growing up in Mexico, I didn't see how it was possible, but I thought to myself, "I will work a lot to be able to go."

When I was 15, I met someone at my job who told me that he knew the road. He asked if I wanted to go, and I said, "Yes, I'll go." But when I asked him the price, it was so much money that I told him I couldn't.

I called my brother-in-law in New York and he told me that if I wanted to go, he would lend me the money. "Of course I want to go," I said. Then I asked the man at my job when I could leave for New York.

"I leave tomorrow," he said.

(Translated from Spanish.)

"Perfect," I told him. "I'll go with you."

I was so excited. I took the first truck to Mexico City at about 4 in the morning. I left without saying goodbye to anyone. I felt bad, but I had to choose between living with tremendous poverty and finding something better for myself.

All my life I'd been trying to work my way out of poverty and free myself from my anger and hurt. My parents abandoned me when I was 2. They left me with my grandparents in a small community, and they left my two older sisters with my aunt in a nearby city. They never sent money (that I know of) or visited.

The community where I lived, Zacualpan in Guerrero state, was very poor. There was no electricity, no streets—only darkness and misery. I grew up hungry, without toys or shoes. If I asked for anything, my grandparents told me I had to make my own money because they had nothing. They also wouldn't allow me to play soccer with other boys my age, and they beat me if I disobeyed.

One day when I was 5 or 6, I decided to run away to live independently and work. I took money that my grandfather had hidden and boarded a bus to Matamoros, a town five hours from my community. For the next few years, I lived with other children and made a living selling candy and shining shoes on the street.

I thought crossing into the U.S. would take only a few days, but our journey lasted weeks.

In Mexico, children live on the streets for many reasons. Some simply want to have a lot of friends and do what they want without anyone telling them they can't. Others have parents who don't care if their children leave because they're very poor, or who think only of themselves and their children don't matter to them. For many poor children, living on the streets is the only way of surviving.

When I was about 8, I moved to another town, Morelia. I was sitting in a park one day when I saw my aunt. She took me in and for a few years I lived with her and my older sisters. But she demanded that I go to school and I was a troublesome child in school, always getting mixed up in problems. After a few years, I left my aunt's house and made my living on the streets once again.

This time, I moved from the small towns of my childhood to the slums of Mexico City. There I sank to the bottom of darkness, getting involved in gangs, hurting many people and getting hurt, too. I was drinking a lot and even using heroin, partly to have fun, and partly to soothe the sadness I felt about being abandoned by my parents.

It was never my intention to become a bad person, but I feel now that I caused a lot of pain and tears.

During those years I also searched for my parents, whose love I believed would save me. I heard they were in Cuernavaca, which is close to Mexico City, so I went there and eventually I met some people who knew them. Through these friends I sent messages to my parents asking them why they had left me and asking to spend time with them. They never answered my questions, only told me that they were too busy working when I wanted to see them.

Every day that passed without seeing them, I grew to hate them. I asked myself, "Why do they never have time for me?" Finally, it hurt too much. I gave up on meeting my parents or speaking to them, and I left for Puebla, a big city far away, where I could live my life without wondering about them each day. I told myself, "The hardest part is behind me. I don't need my parents anymore."

In Puebla I was lucky to find a job selling gum, cigarettes and other little things. The problem was at night. I slept in parks, under bridges and in the markets. When I did well, I slept in the hallways of hotels.

I had all these conflicts and problems on my mind as I began my trip out of Mexico. By the time I arrived in Tijuana I felt confused. So I filled myself with courage and told myself, "God will pardon me. I am going and I will show everyone that I can work hard and become someone."

I didn't know what was waiting for me at the border. It was much worse than I'd imagined. I thought crossing into the U.S. would take only a few days, but our journey lasted weeks. There was tremendous cold at night and insufferable heat by day.

Walking for hours and hours across the desert, I grew hungry and thirsty but ran out of food and water. There were many men waiting along the way to steal my money, and immigration agents searching for illegals like myself.

While the doctors were operating on me, I was dreaming of all the places I most enjoyed—a marvelous countryside, so beautiful that I can't describe it in words. But I woke up to a nightmare.

At times I thought I was dreaming, but I was awake and alone in the middle of a desert. I thought my life had ended, and in those hours when I was lost in the desert I thought about my parents and felt sad that, once more, I was only going farther from them. I thought about my childhood, about the things I had done that were not worth doing.

I knew I couldn't erase the past. I only wished that one day I could speak to my family and try to make things better between us once I arrived in the U.S. Thanks to God, I finally found the correct road, made it to Los Angeles, and with a loan from my brother-in-law, flew to New York.

I arrived in New York on January 3, 2000, full of dreams. I began to work at a restaurant and moved in with people my cousin knew. It was six people in one room. They told me the house rules and I didn't like them—we weren't allowed to smoke or drink in the house.

Soon I found a place where I was allowed to live according to my own rules. Little did I know that would be my downfall. Soon I was back to my old ways, spending all of my time when I wasn't working hanging out with friends.

Life here was harder than I'd imagined. My jobs didn't pay well, I still felt lonely and haunted by my past, and my dreams began to feel further and further away. Soon alcohol became my daily bread, and my friends and I liked heroin, too. It was the only way to make all of my problems disappear.

One day two years ago, I woke up with a terrible headache. I told my roommates that I felt awful but they thought I was joking with them, because I had told them many stories before. So they left for work.

Luckily, another roommate came in from his job soon after and saw me looking very bad. He called 911. It seemed like the ambulance came immediately. After that, I don't remember anything that happened. They told me later they'd thought I was dead.

It turned out I'd had a ruptured aneurysm—bleeding in the brain that can be fatal. (The doctors told me it was probably my heroin use that caused it.)

While the doctors were operating on me, I was dreaming of all the places I most enjoyed—a marvelous countryside, so beautiful that I can't describe it in words. But I woke up to a nightmare. I couldn't talk. I was in the hospital alone. I could barely move and I couldn't walk.

I was in the hospital for an entire year. It was difficult and disgraceful to be confined to a bed. I thought I'd never talk or walk again.

They gave me all kinds of therapy, and I slowly learned to walk again, but only with a cane. My balance isn't good. I can't use my left hand very much, either. And the whole left side of my body is weak.

During my time in the hospital, I said goodbye to all of my dreams. I couldn't believe that I might no longer be able to work or be in control of my future. How would I survive?

At times I thought that if I had stayed in Mexico, perhaps

everything would be different. But I also remembered that I came here to find a better future, so I could climb a little bit out of poverty.

Toward the end of my stay in the hospital, two people from the foster care system came to see me and said they were in charge of my case. They told me, "We're in charge of finding a family where you can live." I was overjoyed.

Soon I moved in with a family that I'm still living with now. The family is helping me a lot. At times I think they're giving me too many things. I feel grateful to them. I also fear how I will live without their support. My physical disabilities make me feel like a child.

I would love to return to my beautiful Mexico—but if it's hard to make a life here as a disabled person, it's worse there.

I believed I would be able to live with the family until I could work again, and I hoped that by being in foster care, I might be able to get citizenship, because there are special laws to help young people in foster care stay in the U.S. legally. But recently, the people at my agency told me that because I'm now 22, I don't have a legal right to be in foster care or to stay in this country.

They told me that I'm probably going to be sent back to Mexico. I don't want to go. It's not that I don't want to visit—I would love to return to my beautiful Mexico—but if it's hard to make a life here as a disabled person, it's worse there. Besides, it's physically very difficult to cross the border. If I go back, I will never return to the U.S. That's very sad.

I'm afraid of what will happen to me in Mexico. I don't have a close relationship with anyone in my family. I'm not sure they'll be willing to help me when I return.

I've talked to my sister in Mexico on the phone a few times. She told me she's made peace with my mother, and once she put my mother on the phone to talk to me. When my mother pronounced my name, I couldn't speak. I stood there in silence, and then I cried. It was the first time I'd ever heard her voice, and she's still never heard mine.

I'm also afraid I may put my family in danger if I stay with them, because my life on the streets gave me enemies. If my enemies want to hurt me by hurting my family, I'll have to leave them and try to survive on my own.

For a long time I was hoping the foster care agency could somehow help me, but recently I met with a lawyer who told me that the agency can't do anything for me. The lawyer told me, "I've asked everybody and they all say the same thing. I can't give you any hope of staying."

Now I feel like I'm going crazy, I'm so sad. I feel that all the hopes and dreams of my life are over. I don't want to plan my return to Mexico. I just want to cry, to disappear. I want to go to sleep and wake up to find that the last few years have been nothing but a dream.

I'm trying to look at the positive that could come out of returning to my country. Maybe it's time for me to confront my past and my parents. This could be my opportunity to learn their motives for abandoning me, and to build a new relationship with my family.

I tell myself that I can't lose my hope, because our hopes are the last things we have. As they say in my country, "A man never gives up." I have to believe that a miracle might happen.

Pedro was 22 when he wrote this story.

Patricia Battles

American at Heart—
But Not on Paper

By Anonymous

The first time I went looking for work I was 15. I went to Modell's sports store because one of my friends had worked there and told me about his experience stocking shoeboxes in the back all by himself. He was like me and didn't like working with customers, so I figured the job would suit me perfectly, keeping me away from obnoxious people.

I grabbed an application from a box near the front entrance of the store. As I rode the escalator to the second level I filled out everything except the box for Social Security number and made my way to the registers.

When I arrived face-to-face with the manager, he said, "Hello sir, welcome to Modell's. My name is Chris. How can I help you today?"

To increase the odds of him liking me, I decided to imitate his formal manner and extended my arm to shake his hand. I introduced myself and said, "I filled out this application in hope of working with people who know how to do their job." I gave a wide grin and placed the application in his hand right side up.

He must have been impressed with the way I handled the situation, because on the spot he looked the application over. It didn't come as a surprise when he pointed out the missing Social Security number, even though I'd hoped he'd ignore it. I made an "Oh, that's what I forgot" gesture, followed by a confident explanation. "I'll bring it in tomorrow since I can never remember numbers properly," I said.

He said I could start training that day, but instead I made up an excuse and said tomorrow would be a better idea. He smirked and told me, "For future reference, try to memorize your Social Security number, since it will haunt you all your life."

I can't take part in the privileges most Americans enjoy, like driving a car or applying for a standard job, because my parents brought me here illegally.

The truth was that I didn't have a Social Security number. As an undocumented Latin-American immigrant, I can't legally work in the United States. I exited the store feeling confident that I could have gotten the job, but also gloomy that I hadn't. I began to realize that my options for getting a job were severely limited.

I arrived in the United States at age 5 with both my parents. People often believe I'm American-born because I don't speak with an accent and my English is a bit better than my Spanish. Though I want to maintain my native culture, I feel "Americanized" because I try to learn from the diverse group of people all around me, from the melting pot of ideas that makes America.

Despite this, I can't take part in the privileges most Americans enjoy, like driving a car or applying for a standard job, because my parents brought me here illegally when I was too young to have a say.

The Modell's manager ended up calling my house and leaving messages that the position was still available and they needed me ASAP. To get him off my back I said I was failing school and couldn't be distracted by a job, but I think he figured out the truth. Before, I had been an eager applicant, but at the mention of "Social Security number" my attitude had completely changed.

I thought my situation was unfair, especially when I saw all my friends working and I wasn't allowed to take the same steps toward independence. No teenager wants to hassle their parents for money for the rest of their life; I needed a job. But jobs that paid off the books didn't have a sign outside that said, "No Social? No problem, we hire!"

I knew I could either dwell on the injustice and do nothing, or be creative. So that winter, I decided to risk catching a flu or fever shoveling snow from people's houses. I walked to Shore Road in Bay Ridge, a wealthy area in Brooklyn where many residents are older and might need shoveling done.

O ver two days, I made around $300 shoveling entire driveways by myself and helping owners who were shoveling outside their homes. In one home, the owners served me hot chocolate and a croissant; in another, I received a $100 check for helping a couple dig out their car. I enjoyed the experience of manual work and meeting generous people, but I knew I couldn't do this all year. I needed to find a more stable source of income.

One of my friends was in charge of handling flyers for jewelry stores, restaurants and cell phone providers. Since he paid in cash we agreed that I would handle one or two routes for minimum wage. But the job was tedious. I had to stand on a street corner handing flyers to passersby. I had to pick up any discarded flyers or I would get money deducted. After a while, I got tired of people throwing the flyers on the ground five feet away from me, so I quit.

Looking at my options, I began to understand that jobs with no set schedule or promised salary would leave me facing uncertainties all the time. But I wanted to buy a bike, so I had to do something.

The friends that I hung out with didn't have jobs but always had money. In my time of need, I realized they could give me a financial boost. I didn't need to ask what they did for money since I already knew. All I did was ask, "Can I help develop more customers?"

I started working with them in the underground economy. Money was abundant and in this job I didn't have to do any hard manual labor or distribute things alone. At first I just passed the word around the school about who sold what item and how great it was. I acted as a walking advertisement, because I was absorbed in the desire to make money.

Jobs that paid off the books didn't have a sign outside that said, 'No Social? No problem, we hire!'

Gradually I began ditching classes to hang out with these people. But I knew I couldn't sustain this lifestyle. Getting caught by the police would jeopardize my entire future—in my situation, the risk was not only jail, but possible deportation.

Besides this, I realized money wasn't the only reason I wanted a job. I also wanted to accomplish something with a larger meaning, not just help people consume things. Once I discovered that there were some things I didn't want to do for money, I stopped communicating with my old friends and decided to change my attitude.

I finally asked my father if I would be able to work with him. I had been reluctant to do this because I had bad childhood memories of him taking me to work with him—I was stubborn and wouldn't listen to him, and I didn't like it when he would yell at me for making a mistake.

Yet as a handyman he's made many good connections, since he does a professional job on construction, electrical and plumbing projects. Working with him again as a teenager reminded me I can always earn an honest living doing what he does.

I also started working in a video game store because I wanted the chance to do something different and, of course, because I would be paid off the books and wouldn't need a Social Security number. More recently, I began advertising my services as a repairman for percussion instruments in online forums. The ads have brought me a few jobs so far, and I'm hoping to develop my craftsman skills and one day turn my hobby into a steady income.

But the video store underwent a change in management a few weeks ago, and the new bosses wanted all employees to bring in their legal documents and appear on the store's payroll, so that was the end of that job.

I've gotten so used to these frustrations that they're not a big deal anymore. I know if I want a job all I have to do is look harder than most people. I see this as less of a headache than you might expect, because I believe my efforts make me stronger all the time. By

I don't want to do any job that comes my way just to get by.

using these experiences to increase my determination, I can take control of my life, instead of believing that because of my parents' decisions I'm condemned.

I haven't had much time to think about my plans for long-term work, since I've been busy trying to finish high school. Besides, in many ways I've lived as an American almost my entire life, so immigration problems don't always seem real. My dream is to become a teacher, because I want to help develop not only good students, but good citizens. But it will be hard to pursue such meaningful employment without documentation.

It would be disappointing to have to relinquish my goals just because I need to make money to support myself; I don't want to do any job that comes my way just to get by. But my other options are to move back to a country that is practically foreign to me, or live life under a fake identity and face more problems. So I'll do what I have to do to survive, but I'm also going to look for ways to make my life fulfilling.

I will attend community college, continue to learn from people I meet, and volunteer around my neighborhood. My desire is to contribute to society and help my community prosper, and in this sense I don't need to be a citizen to be a good American or find satisfaction in what I do.

The author was 19 when he wrote this story.

Teodoro Romero

The Daily News Taught Me English

By Angel Ortiz

"Get your newspapers," said Mrs. Castañeda, my 8th grade English as a Second Language (ESL) teacher.

"Newspapers again? Who cares about that trash?" I thought, sitting at my back-row desk. I didn't care about newspaper reports of local murders or far-away wars.

I looked around, trying to find another student who'd want to use the newspaper as a weapon to play-hit each other. But my search was useless. Everyone else was following her directions and reading the *New York Daily News*.

Most of the time reading put me to sleep. But since there was nothing else to do, I ended up following the crowd and reading my newspaper.

I never thought my life in New York City would be so boring.

Back in Mexico, where I lived until three years ago, my life was such a party. I went to school from 1-6 p.m. but only to play and bully people.

At school in Mexico, the teachers rarely bothered me. They didn't care if I read the textbooks, and most of the time, I didn't. When I did do the work, I only enjoyed working independently. I'd do the work the way I wanted without asking anyone's opinion or caring about my grades.

After school, I'd go to the arcade with my friends to play video games. I hoped to grow up and study for a career like a lawyer or a doctor where I could earn a high salary. I didn't understand back then that studying for those careers wouldn't be as easy as winning a soccer match or getting a good grade in school.

But life got hard when I was 14. My mother and I moved to New York to join my father, who'd moved here to find better-paying work when I was 3 years old. He had a job at a restaurant and only visited us once every couple of years.

I didn't really know my father so I didn't know if I missed him. That worried my mother, who decided to move to the U.S. so I'd get to know him better. I also thought it might be a good idea to move to "the land of opportunity," where I dreamed I could succeed economically.

Before I moved I knew that people in the U.S. spoke English. But honestly, I didn't stop to analyze the situation when I was packing to leave. Just like I assumed I could easily become a doctor or a lawyer, I assumed that I had the skills to learn English in a few weeks.

When I arrived in the U.S. and started 8th grade in Brooklyn, New York, everyone was speaking an alien language I couldn't understand. I'd never lived anywhere where everybody spoke a different language than me, and I was shocked. I wished that life had subtitles, like in foreign movies.

And school was such a serious place here. Sometimes I felt

like I was in a geek class. The teachers were always watching my moves so I couldn't even throw a paper ball at a classmate's head. And the worst thing was having to read that stupid newspaper.

But after almost seven months of complaining about everything, I realized that complaining didn't change things. It just made my life worse. If I was going to survive in this new concrete jungle, I had to adapt.

I needed to learn English, so I began reading the newspaper on my own after school. Sometimes I got so bored that I threw it away. But after about four months, I started enjoying reading the crime and sports stories.

I hated to admit it but my ESL teacher was right about reading newspapers. They really boosted my understanding of English. I remember trying to picture simple words from the paper such as "sky," "tree" and "grass" in my head. I tried to save

Everyone was speaking an alien language I couldn't understand. I wished that life had subtitles, like in foreign movies.

them in my head along with the meaning usually given by my teacher. The next time that I read an article, I understood it better. My teachers noticed my improvement and moved me into a more advanced English class.

After six months of studying, I could go to the store and ask for things that I wanted to buy without any frustration. I could understand the lyrics of songs that I'd liked on the radio but not understood before. For the first time I felt like I was living on earth again because I didn't hear alien babbling. I could understand people.

Although I used the paper to learn English, I also started caring about what the newspapers were reporting about the world. In Mexico, I didn't really care about anything but not feeling bored. Here I started reading about economics, war, discrimination, hunger, violence and plenty more.

The newspaper was my window into the cruelty of our world. After a while, the stories seemed to repeat but with different characters: headlines about the war in Iraq, people being killed on the streets of New York, parents beating their kids to death, people fighting about almost everything in the courts, people from different cultures trying and sometimes failing to get along. It wasn't the goofy, playful life I'd led in Mexico.

After I started reading about so many different topics, I also started learning from my friends at Brooklyn International HS, a school for recent immigrants from all over the world. They helped make me more aware of how many different people there are. I never would have met people so different from me at my school in Mexico, where almost everyone was the same race and religion.

*E*ven goofing off with my friends has turned into a lesson on religious dietary restrictions. One day some friends and I went to the beach to play at the arcade. Everyone decided to get some snacks except Mo (not his real name). I thought Mo was just being cheap. When we began to eat our hot dogs and sodas, Mo wouldn't eat anything even though we offered him some.

"No thanks," he kept saying every time that we offered.

"Are you on a diet? Allergic? Or you just hate hot dogs?" I said, joking with him.

"No, nothing like that, man. I can't eat pork."

Mo told me that he was Muslim and from Yemen, and that his religion doesn't allow people to eat pork. I was impressed by how strongly he followed his beliefs. We insisted for more than 20 minutes, but he wouldn't eat a hot dog.

Coming to the U.S. was an awakening after living in my little party world in Mexico, where hanging out with my crew on the streets was the only thing I cared about. Back then I considered everything else simply not my business. I let life pass by without stopping to look at the bigger picture. If I had stayed in Mexico, I might not ever have changed.

I have to give thanks to my bossy ESL teacher for making me read the paper and forcing me to pay attention to the world around me. It opened up my mind and taught me about the imperfection of our world, the challenges that people face every day and the variety of people in the world. I also give thanks to my friends for teaching me about their cultures and customs. And finally, I have to thank New York City for helping me grow and change.

Once in a while I miss Mexico. I miss the street where I used to hang out with my pals. I miss the crazy stuff that I used to do in school like throwing paper balls and playing jokes on my classmates without getting in trouble. I miss the awesome food, especially the tacos.

But looking at how I've changed, I'm glad I came to New York City. I believe that living here has given me a big taste of the world. Now I don't just dream of economic success. I've learned that there are a lot of problems like discrimination and world hunger that need solutions. I'm still not sure how I'm going to help. But because of what I've learned here, I now dream of finding a way to help our world become a better place.

Angel was in high school when he wrote this story.

Townsend Press

Brothers in Arms

I'm standing in front of Bluford High School, blood on my elbows, gash on my head. My ribs feel cracked. The school is crowded, and I'm three hours late.

I wish I could cut again.

Ms. Spencer, our school principal, will bust me for sure if I go in now. She's heard enough from the other teachers about me, Martin Luna, the dangerous kid from the barrio who used to go to Zamora High. Last time I was in her office, she just stared at me, judging me, her eyes beaming like a cop's spotlight.

"What's the problem between you and Steve Morris?" she asked.

"Nothin'," I said. Even though I hate the kid, I ain't a rat.

She crossed her arms and sighed, still looking at me as if I was some kind a puzzle. I could see she was losing patience. I don't blame her. I ain't easy to deal with. Still, I stared back at her

---

Here's the first chapter from *Brothers in Arms*, by Paul Langan and Ben Alirez, a fictional novel about teens facing difficult situations, like the ones in this book. *Brothers in Arms* is one of several books in the *Bluford Series*™ by Townsend Press.

until she was forced to look away. You can't stare me down. I've been hit by people who would scare you on the street. I don't run from anyone, not principals or kids like Steve Morris who give me trouble. That's part of my problem.

But I ran this morning. I bolted like the roaches in the basement of our old apartment when you turned the light on them. Back in the day, me and my brother would chase them into the shadows, though Huero would never stomp them like me. He was always a good kid. I miss him so much.

What I ran from wasn't no kid. It wasn't the police or a gang. It was bigger than that, and I am not sure running is even gonna save me. And all I got right now is this school that can't handle me and the words my English teacher, Mr. Mitchell, said yesterday.

"Martin, you are talented, and you could have a bright future ahead of you. Don't throw it away. When you feel things getting out of hand, when you know you're getting over your head, talk to me. I'm here for you. I mean that."

I shrugged off his words when he said them. But now I'm hoping they're true, 'cause I feel like I'm bein' swept away. I'm over my head. I realized it this morning, but it's been happening for months, years actually. Now I gotta make a choice.

I see the security guard at the door watching me. He's talking to someone on a radio. Ms. Spencer is on her way out to me. This is it.

What should I do?

All this started on July 10th. I remember exactly what happened because I still dream about it. Sometimes I wake up in the middle of the night covered in sweat, my heart jumping against my ribs. I'm never gonna forget.

Me and my four homeboys were hanging out in the alley behind my friend Frankie's house. We were watching him wax his 1972 Pontiac LeMans. Chrome wheels and as blue as the ocean, the car was Frankie's baby. If you asked him, he'd say he treated it better than any person. It's true.

The southern California sun was beating down on us, making the concrete so hot the bottoms of our shoes got soft and sticky, but we had music from the car stereo. And Chago, one of our boys, had a case of beer. I never drank the stuff because I saw what it did to my father, and what he did when he was drunk, but Chago was different. He liked his beer, and he didn't get too out of hand, so it was all good.

We were just kicking it, talking cars and girls, when Frankie looked at me and Chago.

"Homies, I gotta find me a chick. I spend way too much time with you lowlifes," Frankie said.

We laughed. Frankie Pacheco was the toughest guy in our crew. He also got in the most trouble. There were lots of rumors about things Frankie had done, but he never talked about them unless he was drunk, and then you couldn't listen to him. A scar on his left side marked where someone had stabbed him last summer. I was there that day backing him up. I watched Frankie kick the kid with the knife in the stomach and face. Frankie knew how to handle himself. He was nineteen, three years older than me. Other people might've had problems with him. But we thought he was family.

"Dude, you're dreaming," I teased, throwing a light punch his way. "You ever look in the mirror?"

Junie cracked up and nearly spit out a mouthful of beer onto Frankie's car. He was always laughing at something.

Frankie punched me right back, the hit glancing off my shoulder. The two of us always pretended to fight. Though we never said anything about it, I think we both knew there was a serious edge to it.

"Hey, Martin," said Jesus, one of the other guys. He was puffing a cigarette. It made him stink like my father. "I got Huero at 11:00."

I swung around in time to see a small figure ducking behind

a green metal dumpster the size of a pickup truck. It was Huero, my eight year old brother. Huero's real name was Eric. Huero was just his nickname, a Spanish word that means *light-skinned*. We called him that since he was a little kid 'cause his skin was paler than mine and my mom's.

"He's back again?" Frankie asked, shaking his head and dropping his fists. Frankie didn't like many things, especially kids. "I don't know *nobody* who worships someone like that little brother of yours worships you."

It was true. Huero had a habit of following me, no matter where I was or what I was doing. It was frustrating and I tried to discourage it. I mean, how do you deal with someone who looks up to you like, well, like a big brother?

I wasn't always the best at dealing with him, but I didn't want him around, especially when we were drinking or checking out girls. It isn't cool to have your little brother there when you're try-ing to get a girl's phone number. And I didn't want him around the cigarettes and the alcohol. He would see that on his own in a few years, I thought. I was wrong.

"Make sure you take care of your brother," my mom said earlier that day. Most of the time, I did that by sending him away, making up lies to get him to leave. Anything that gave me more time with the boys.

"Huero!" I barked, stepping away from Frankie's lowrider. "Come out of there."

Huero came out from behind the dumpster a second later, pushing along his squeaky, weather-beaten bicycle. He took that bike everywhere.

"What did I tell you about following me?"

"Sorry, Marty," he stammered. "I just—"

"You just what?" I prodded. "You know you're not supposed to be here."

With puppy-dog eyes, he looked over at the boys and ignored me. "Hi, guys, I got some gum. I can share it with you."

Chago and Frankie shook their heads at me and glanced away embarrassed.

"Go home, Huero—*now!*" I ordered.

My brother stared at me then. Just for a second, but long enough for me to see his disappointment. All the kid wanted was to be with me, and there I was sending him away.

"Okay, Marty," he said, sounding defeated. "I'll see you later then, okay?"

"Yeah, yeah," I said with a nod, feeling guilty for chasing him away. I couldn't stay mad at Huero for long. And no matter how bad I treated him, he just kept coming back to me with those eyes. The kid looked at me like I was a superhero or something. *Me.* He was too young to know better.

I watched him for a second as he began to pedal away, and then I turned around. "Brothers! Did I tell you guys what he said this morning?" I asked.

"What's that?"

"Huero said he wants to be just like me when he gets older. Can you believe that?" The idea seemed silly to me then. Now it haunts me.

We all laughed, but then we heard Huero shouting in the distance.

"*Marty!*"

I turned back to see him pedaling my way as fast as he could.

A half block behind him, a white sedan was speeding down the alley in our direction. Something was sticking out of the window. It glinted in the bright sunlight.

"Watch out, Marty," Huero yelled. My little brother was trying to protect *me.*

The car raced toward us, its windshield tinted so I couldn't get a good look inside. Huero was pedaling fast, but the car was coming faster. I yelled for him to get out of the way, but he wasn't rushing for cover. He could have hid behind the dumpster, or he could have darted to the side of the street. But instead Huero came toward me, his big brown eyes wide open and unblinking as he pedaled, the bike squeaking like a field of crickets.

Chago, Jesus, and Frankie were scrambling behind the low-rider. I could hear their shoes scraping the concrete.

"Get down, homes!" Frankie yelled.

Then the shots rang out.

Pop! Pop! Pop! They sounded like loud firecrackers, but the smell was different, more crisp, like the smell of burning matches. The kind that burns the inside of your nose.

Huero reached me, leaping from his bike into my arms as the car approached. I didn't have time to think. I just grabbed him and turned so that my body covered his like a shield.

More shots rang out. A bullet zinged past my ear. Another hit the sidewalk and rocketed into a window somewhere. I can still hear the glass breaking in my dreams. Then, just as suddenly, the bullets stopped. Looking back over my shoulder, I saw the car turning the corner, its wheels squealing like some kind of demon.

"They're gone, dude," said Frankie. He stepped out from behind the Le Mans.

My heart was about to jump out of my chest. I'd heard gunshots, and I'd seen a store after a shooting. But I'd never been shot at before. I took a deep breath when I was sure they were gone.

"It's okay now, Huero." I said. My little brother looked like he was sleeping. I almost didn't want to bother him. "Huero?" I repeated.

The guys rushed to my side as I remained kneeling.

"Come on little buddy, wake up. What's the matter?" I put my arm under him to sit him up, and I felt the wetness in my hand. It was warm, like bathwater, but it was coming out the back of his head.

"Martin, it don't look like he's breathing," Chago said softly. The tone of his voice alarmed me 'cause Chago never talked like that.

"Oh, no," Junie said.

My vision was breaking up like I was seeing the world through shattered glass. My hands were red, and my little brother's life was spilling out onto the street, mixing with the soil like rain.

This wasn't happening. It couldn't be. Not to my brother.

"Come on, Huero," I said, rocking him like I did when he was little. "Come on."

People were starting to gather around , but I blocked them out. Huero was going to wake up. He had to.

I touched his cheek. He was still warm, and his skin was soft like when he was a baby. But my fingers left smudges of blood on his face, and his body was limp. "Wake up for your big brother," I said. "Wake up!"

A woman screamed in the crowd behind me, and then I heard a voice.

"Call an ambulance! That boy's been shot."

I couldn't talk or move or think. I just sat there on the ground holding my little brother.

Someone put an arm on my shoulder. I turned to see Frankie there, his eyes dark and stormy, his brow rumpled like a dented car.

"We'll get them, homes," he said. "We'll get them." He patted me on the shoulder and walked away. I heard the sirens screaming closer then.

I couldn't let go of Huero when the medics arrived. They had to pull me away because I wasn't going to give up on my little brother. But inside, I knew he was gone. And, in a way, so was I.

Whoever shot him tore a hole through my heart too, a black hole that, instead of blood, gushed only a desire for revenge. And as I endured the trip to the hospital, the sound of my mother wailing at the top of her lungs, the sight of my brother's blood spilling into the sink when I washed my hands, that desire grew like a tumor.

That was two months ago.

Brothers in Arms, *a Bluford Series™ novel, is reprinted with permission from Townsend Press. Copyright © 2002.*

Want to read more? This and other *Bluford Series™* novels and paperbacks can be purchased for $1 each at www.townsendpress.com.

Teens:
How to Get More Out of This Book

Self-help: The teens who wrote the stories in this book did so because they hope that telling their stories will help readers who are facing similar challenges. They want you to know that you are not alone, and that taking specific steps can help you manage or overcome very difficult situations. They've done their best to be clear about the actions that worked for them so you can see if they'll work for you.

Writing: You can also use the book to improve your writing skills. Each teen in this book wrote 5-10 drafts of his or her story before it was published. If you read the stories closely you'll see that the teens work to include a beginning, a middle, and an end, and good scenes, description, dialogue, and anecdotes (little stories). To improve your writing, take a look at how these writers construct their stories. Try some of their techniques in your own writing.

Reading: Finally, you'll notice that we include the first chapter from a Bluford Series novel in this book, alongside the true stories by teens. We hope you'll like it enough to continue reading. The more you read, the more you'll strengthen your reading skills. Teens at Youth Communication like the Bluford novels because they explore themes similar to those in their own stories. Your school may already have the Bluford books. If not, you can order them online for only $1.

Resources on the Web

We will occasionally post Think About It questions on our website, www.youthcomm.org, to accompany stories in this and other Youth Communication books. We try out the questions with teens and post the ones they like best. Many teens report that writing answers to those questions in a journal is very helpful.

How to Use This Book in Staff Training

Staff say that reading these stories gives them greater insight into what teens are thinking and feeling, and new strategies for working with them. You can help the staff you work with by using these stories as case studies.

Select one story to read in the group, and ask staff to identify and discuss the main issue facing the teen. There may be disagreement about this, based on the background and experience of staff. That is fine. One point of the exercise is that teens have complex lives and needs. Adults can probably be more effective if they don't focus too narrowly and can see several dimensions of their clients.

Ask staff: What issues or feelings does the story provoke in them? What kind of help do they think the teen wants? What interventions are likely to be most promising? Least effective? Why? How would you build trust with the teen writer? How have other adults failed the teen, and how might that affect his or her willingness to accept help? What other resources would be helpful to this teen, such as peer support, a mentor, counseling, family therapy, etc.

Resources on the Web

From time to time we will post Think About It questions on our website, www.youthcomm.org, to accompany stories in this and other Youth Communication books. We try out the questions with teens and post the ones that they find most effective. We'll also post lesson for some of the stories. Adults can use the questions and lessons in workshops.

Teachers and Staff:
How to Use This Book in Groups

When working with teens individually or in groups, using these stories can help young people face difficult issues in a way that feels safe to them. That's because talking about the issues in the stories usually feels safer to teens than talking about those same issues in their own lives. Addressing issues through the stories allows for some personal distance; they hit close to home, but not too close. Talking about them opens up a safe place for reflection. As teens gain confidence talking about the issues in the stories, they usually become more comfortable talking about those issues in their own lives.

Below are general questions that can help you lead discussions about the stories, which help teens and staff reflect on the issues in their own work and lives. In most cases you can read a story and conduct a discussion in one 45-minute session. Teens are usually happy to read the stories aloud, with each teen reading a paragraph or two. (Allow teens to pass if they don't want to read.) It takes 10-15 minutes to read a story straight through. However, it is often more effective to let workshop participants make comments and discuss the story as you go along. The workshop leader may even want to annotate her copy of the story beforehand with key questions.

If teens read the story ahead of time or silently, it's good to break the ice with a few questions that get everyone on the same page: Who is the main character? How old is she? What happened to her? How did she respond? Etc. Another good starting question is: "What stood out for you in the story?" Go around the room and let each person briefly mention one thing.

Then move on to open-ended questions, which encourage participants to think more deeply about what the writers were feeling, the choices they faced, and they actions they took. There are no right or wrong answers to the open-ended questions. Open-ended questions encourage participants to think about how the themes, emotions and choices in the stories relate to their own lives. Here are some examples of open-ended questions that we have found to be effective. You can use variations of these questions with almost any story in this book.

—What main problem or challenge did the writer face?

—What choices did the teen have in trying to deal with the problem?

—Which way of dealing with the problem was most effective for the teen? Why?

—What strengths, skills, or resources did the teen use to address the challenge?

—If you were in the writer's shoes, what would you have done?

—What could adults have done better to help this young person?

—What have you learned by reading this story that you didn't know before?

—What, if anything, will you do differently after reading this story?

—What surprised you in this story?

—Do you have a different view of this issue, or see a different way of dealing with it, after reading this story? Why or why not?

Credits

The stories in this book originally appeared in the following Youth Communication publications:

"Penguin in the Sahara," by Sayda Morales, *New Youth Connections*, March 2009

"Black? Latina? Don't Ask Me to Choose," by Charika Martin, *New Youth Connections*, March 2005

"Caught in a Tug of War," by David Miranda, *New Youth Connections*, December 1992

"When Merengue Is Just Not Enough," by Karina Sang, *New Youth Connections*, March 1992

"Showin' Off My Flag All Proud," by Omar Morales, *New Youth Connections*, May/June 1998

"Don't Call Me Puerto Rican," by Janill Briones, *New Youth Connections*, March 2004

"No Poofy Quinceañera Dress for Me," by Daniela Castillo, *New Youth Connections*, January/February 2007

"I Hated Myself," by David Miranda, *New Youth Connections*, April 1993

"Grandma, I Love You," by Daniel Rosado, *New Youth Connections*, May/June 1994

"What I Learned from Roberto Clemente," by Luis Reyes, *New Youth Connections*, April 1998

"The Young Lords: Rebels with a Cause," by David Miranda, *New Youth Connections*, June 1993

"Los Buitres, Roadblocks, and Mayan Ruins," by Sheila Maldonado, *New Youth Connections*, June 1991

"Leaving 'El Combito,'" by Angy Gonzalez, *New Youth Connections*, April 2005

"Torn Between Two Countries," by Anghela Calvo, *New Youth Connections*, April 2002

"Learning to Love My Bolivian Culture," by Anghela Calvo, *New Youth Connections*, April 2002

"Can I Have Both?" by Fanny Brito, *New Youth Connections*, September/October 2003

"Lost in the Desert," by Pedro Cruz, *New Youth Connections*, May/June 2006

"American at Heart—But Not on Paper," by Anonymous, *New Youth Connections*, May/June 2008

"*The Daily News* Taught Me English," by Angel Ortiz, *New Youth Connections*, September/October 2007

About
Youth Communication

Youth Communication, founded in 1980, is a nonprofit youth development program located in New York City whose mission is to teach writing, journalism, and leadership skills. The teenagers we train become writers for our websites and books and for two print magazines, *New Youth Connections*, a general-interest youth magazine, and *Represent*, a magazine by and for young people in foster care.

Each year, up to 100 young people participate in Youth Communication's school-year and summer journalism workshops where they work under the direction of full-time professional editors. Most are African American, Latino, or Asian, and many are recent immigrants. The opportunity to reach their peers with accurate portrayals of their lives and important self-help information motivates the young writers to create powerful stories.

Our goal is to run a strong youth development program in which teens produce high quality stories that inform and inspire their peers. Doing so requires us to be sensitive to the complicated lives and emotions of the teen participants while also providing an intellectually rigorous experience. We achieve that goal in the writing/teaching/editing relationship, which is the core of our program.

Our teaching and editorial process begins with discussions

between adult editors and the teen staff. In those meetings, the teens and the editors work together to identify the most important issues in the teens' lives and to figure out how those issues can be turned into stories that will resonate with teen readers.

Once story topics are chosen, students begin the process of crafting their stories. For a personal story, that means revisiting events in one's past to understand their significance for the future. For a commentary, it means developing a logical and persuasive point of view. For a reported story, it means gathering information through research and interviews. Students look inward and outward as they try to make sense of their experiences and the world around them and find the points of intersection between personal and social concerns. That process can take a few weeks or a few months. Stories frequently go through ten or more drafts as students work under the guidance of their editors, the way any professional writer does.

Many of the students who walk through our doors have uneven skills, as a result of poor education, living under extremely stressful conditions, or coming from homes where English is a second language. Yet, to complete their stories, students must successfully perform a wide range of activities, including writing and rewriting, reading, discussion, reflection, research, interviewing, and typing. They must work as members of a team and they must accept individual responsibility. They learn to provide constructive criticism, and to accept it. They engage in explorations of truthfulness, fairness, and accuracy. They meet deadlines. They must develop the audacity to believe that they have something important to say and the humility to recognize that saying it well is not a process of instant gratification. Rather, it usually requires a long, hard struggle through many discussions and much rewriting.

It would be impossible to teach these skills and dispositions as separate, disconnected topics, like grammar, ethics, or assertiveness. However, we find that students make rapid progress when they are learning skills in the context of an inquiry that is personally significant to them and that will benefit their peers.

When teens publish their stories—in *New Youth Connections* and *Represent,* on the web, and in other publications—they reach tens of thousands of teen and adult readers. Teachers, counselors, social workers, and other adults circulate the stories to young people in their classes and out-of-school youth programs. Adults tell us that teens in their programs—including many who are ordinarily resistant to reading—clamor for the stories. Teen readers report that the stories give them information they can't get anywhere else, and inspire them to reflect on their lives and open lines of communication with adults.

Writers usually participate in our program for one semester, though some stay much longer. Years later, many of them report that working here was a turning point in their lives—that it helped them acquire the confidence and skills that they needed for success in college and careers. Scores of our graduates have overcome tremendous obstacles to become journalists, writers, and novelists. They include National Book Award finalist Edwidge Danticat, novelist Ernesto Quinonez, writer Veronica Chambers and *New York Times* reporter Rachel Swarns. Hundreds more are working in law, business, and other careers. Many are teachers, principals, and youth workers, and several have started nonprofit youth programs themselves and work as mentors— helping another generation of young people develop their skills and find their voices.

Youth Communication is a nonprofit educational corporation. Contributions are gratefully accepted and are tax deductible to the fullest extent of the law.

To make a contribution, or for information about our publications and programs, including our catalog of over 100 books and curricula for hard-to-reach teens, see www.youthcomm.org

About The Editors

Hope Vanderberg was the editor of *New Youth Connections*, Youth Communication's magazine by and for New York City teens, from 2004 to 2008.

Prior to working at Youth Communication, Vanderberg specialized in science journalism and environmental education. She was an editor at Medscape.com, a medical website, wrote articles for *Audubon* and *The Sciences* magazines, and taught children and teens at environmental education centers in California and Texas. She has also worked as a field biologist, studying bird behavior in Puerto Rico.

She has a master's degree in science and environmental journalism from New York University and a bachelor's degree from Earlham College. She is currently a freelance editor.

Keith Hefner co-founded Youth Communication in 1980 and has directed it ever since. He is the recipient of the Luther P. Jackson Education Award from the New York Association of Black Journalists and a MacArthur Fellowship. He was also a Revson Fellow at Columbia University.

Laura Longhine is the editorial director at Youth Communication. She edited *Represent*, Youth Communication's magazine by and for youth in foster care, for three years, and has written for a variety of publications. She has a BA in English from Tufts University and an MS in Journalism from Columbia University.

More Helpful Books From Youth Comunication

 *The Struggle to Be Strong: True Stories by Teens About Overcoming Tough Times.* Foreword by Veronica Chambers. Help young people identify and build on their own strengths with 30 personal stories about resiliency. (Free Spirit)

Starting With "I": Personal Stories by Teenagers. "Who am I and who do I want to become?" Thirty-five stories examine this question through the lens of race, ethnicity, gender, sexuality, family, and more. Increase this book's value with the free Teacher's Guide, available from youthcomm.org. (Youth Communication)

 Real Stories, Real Teens. Inspire teens to read and recognize their strengths with this collection of 26 true stories by teens. The young writers describe how they overcame significant challenges and stayed true to themselves. Also includes the first chapters from three novels in the Bluford Series. (Youth Communication)

The Courage to Be Yourself: True Stories by Teens About Cliques, Conflicts, and Overcoming Peer Pressure. In 26 first-person stories, teens write about their lives with searing honesty. These stories will inspire young readers to reflect on their own lives, work through their problems, and help them discover who they really are. (Free Spirit)

 *Out With It: Gay and Straight Teens Write About Homosexuality.* Break stereotypes and provide support with this unflinching look at gay life from a teen's perspective. With a focus on urban youth, this book also includes several heterosexual teens' transformative experiences with gay peers. (Youth Communication)

Things Get Hectic: Teens Write About the Violence That Surrounds Them. Violence is commonplace in many teens' lives, be it bullying, gangs, dating, or family relationships. Hear the experiences of victims, perpetrators, and witnesses through more than 50 real-world stories. (Youth Communication)

From Dropout to Achiever: Teens Write About School. Help teens overcome the challenges of graduating, which may involve overcoming family problems, bouncing back from a bad semester, or dropping out for a time. These teens show how they achieve academic success. (Youth Communication)

 My Secret Addiction: Teens Write About Cutting. These true accounts of cutting, or self-mutilation, offer a window into the personal and family situations that lead to this secret habit, and show how teens can get the help they need. (Youth Communication)

Sticks and Stones: Teens Write About Bullying. Shed light on bullying, as told from the perspectives of the perpetrator, the victim, and the witness. These stories show why bullying occurs, the harm it causes, and how it might be prevented. (Youth Communication)

 *Boys to Men: Teens Write About Becoming a Man.* The young men in this book write about their confusion, ideals, and the challenges of becoming a man. Their honesty and courage make them role models for teens who are bombarded with contradictory messages about what it means to be a man. (Youth Communication)

Through Thick and Thin: Teens Write About Obesity, Eating Disorders and Self Image. Help teens who struggle with obesity, eating disorders and body weight issues. These stories show the pressures teens face when they are confronted by unrealistic standards for physical appearance, and how emotions can affect the way we eat. (Youth Communication)

To order these and other books, go to:
www.youthcomm.org
or call 212-279-0708 x115

CPSIA information
Printed in the USA
BVOW04s2207080

352912BV0